HOW TO MAKE SPEECHES
FOR ALL OCCASIONS

Also by Harold P. Zelko

BUSINESS AND PROFESSIONAL SPEECH
COMMUNICATION
(*With Frank Dance*)

COMMUNICATIVE SPEAKING AND LISTENING
(*With Robert Oliver and Paul Holtzman*)

THE BUSINESS CONFERENCE

BELL SYSTEM SPEAKER'S MANUAL

HOW TO BECOME A SUCCESSFUL SPEAKER

Also by Marjorie E. Zelko

Ed., ENCYCLOPEDIA OF WORLD TRAVEL,
NEW REVISED EDITION

How to Make Speeches for All Occasions

A Practical Guide and Workbook for
Preparing for All Speaking Responsibilities

By
HAROLD P. ZELKO
and
MARJORIE E. ZELKO

Garden City, New York
DOUBLEDAY & COMPANY, INC.

To
Jeremy, Rachel, Deborah, and Claudia,
and whatever other speakers come along . . .

CONTENTS

3

THE SUBSTANCE OF YOUR SPEECH

4

YOU AS A COMMUNICATOR

5

OTHER SPEAKING AND GROUP SITUATIONS

WORKBOOK FOR BETTER SPEAKING

PREFACE

This is a book about speechmaking. And, more basically, it is a book about how to communicate—to speak, listen, interact, and understand. Few needs are as great as the need for communication, and few means of communication are as rewarding as speaking to or with others.

We are assuming that you have been called upon to make a speech, chair a meeting, run a conference, or some similar function. Or perhaps you had been asked but refused because you were afraid to face an audience and be a speaker. Or maybe you hope you'll be giving a talk at some future date on a subject that particularly interests you. At any rate, you are interested in learning how to make a speech and how to prepare yourself to be at ease before an audience.

Our aim is to help you build a strong foundation. Once you are familiar with the basic steps in speechmaking they will become part of your thought processes. Actually, most of the principles of good speaking are as important in a personal conversation with a friend as they are in a large meeting hall. Read this book carefully, and you will find your confidence growing on all levels of speaking.

Our belief is that you should be as close to your natural self as you can be when you speak, but that you should refine your normal speech habits by carefully planning and preparing. Your speech will be more meaningful to the audience but will come across with the ease of an enlarged conversation.

Following the text section of the book, in which you will

learn all the methods and techniques of speechmaking, we have written a workbook filled with more than fifty speech outlines on a wide variety of topics. They will show you the many ways to organize and develop your speech. Refer to them often, for you may find one very close to a subject on which you plan to speak. In addition, there are tips, check questions, source materials, and other important aids in the workbook.

We especially want to thank Seth Goldstein, Gary Zelko, and Sarah Zelko for their help and encouragement.

Making a speech is a rewarding experience and more important today than it ever has been. We hope that this book will be a new and unique contribution to all your communication goals.

Harold P. Zelko
Marjorie E. Zelko

1

Your Speaking Responsibilities

I. YOU NEED TO COMMUNICATE

II. WHAT KIND OF SPEAKER DO YOU
WANT TO BE?

I

YOU NEED TO COMMUNICATE

You have all it takes to become the next president of the United States, but you must do something to improve your public speaking.

—Herbert Hoover to Thomas Dewey

In this time of corporate giants, computerized billing, and impersonal service, being able to communicate is more important than ever. To separate *you* from the masses, you have to be heard and understood, especially in business. Few frustrations top the feeling of being a small, anonymous cog in the fast-moving wheel of our hurried times.

With so many people competing for good jobs, promotions, offices in organizations, or political posts—be it town clerk or senator—you need to be the articulate, confident one: the person who can stand before a group of people and clearly, confidently give a well-organized talk. Nothing makes a better impression than an effective speaker in day-to-day conversation, in conferences, as a chairmn, or making a speech.

This is a book about speaking, listening, and speechmaking, all inseparable in the process of human communication. Just picking it up makes you take a major step toward improving yourself as a communicator, for it proves your interest in this objective. By reading it carefully, you will learn the essential principles and knowledge needed to develop yourself as a speaker-communicator. By practicing and applying these principles, you can be as effective a speaker as you want to be. This is not something you are born with; it comes by hard work and application.

You have to decide how important communication is to you,

and whether you will apply yourself to become a better speaker. "Speaker" does not mean orator, actor, or performer. It means building upon your own natural manner—using sound principles and methods to become the kind of speaker *you* want to be.

Today's communicating society

You probably spend more time listening or speaking than in any endeavor except breathing. Human interaction is a vital life function. And speech is *not* just something you deliver from a lectern before an audience.

No matter how much time you spend reading, writing, listening to radio, television, or a tape recorder, you as a human being have strong needs to *talk* to people, have your opinions heard, discuss and analyze everything from a book you've read to a new way to grow tomatoes. Talking and understanding adds to confidence and a sense of security often missing today.

Informal communication is the most personal way of interacting. How do you communicate with your family? A service station attendant? Your doctor? Can you clearly get your point across or are you continually frustrated because you know just what you want to explain but can't quite express yourself? One of the primary aims of this book is to help you think clearly and to verbalize your ideas with assurance.

Business communication is probably more important today than it ever was. Like it or not, it's one concrete way to measure a person. Can he express himself? What are his ideas? What can he do for our firm?

Peter Drucker, noted management consultant, wrote: "As soon as you move one step up from the bottom, your effectiveness depends on your ability to reach others through the spoken or written word. And the further away your job is from manual work, the larger the organization of which you are an employee, the more important it will be that you know how to convey your thoughts in writing or speaking. In the very large organizations, whether it is the Government, the large business corporation, or the army, this ability to express oneself is perhaps the most important of all the skills a man can possess."

In today's complex business structure, internal communication is a constant and primary concern, with direct personal contacts through speech playing a dominant part.

Not only *within* a corporation are one's speaking abilities necessary, but an employee—especially at the management level—is often called upon to address groups on the outside, as companies more and more rely on speeches to relate directly with the public and to improve customer relations.

Rather than maintain a rule of secrecy, companies want to be understood. They send out speakers to enhance their reputation, announce a new venture, take a stand on a controversial issue. What effect will his company's new waste disposal system have on the nearby waterways? How can a speaker best explain his corporation's local expansion plans or its decision to relocate? The executive who can succinctly, sincerely, competently represent his firm is invaluable.

Corporations, realizing the need for good speakers, are setting up programs within their firms to teach speech communication. Arthur H. Walsh, Community Relations Supervisor of American Telephone and Telegraph, says, "We now must turn to asking, what can we do to improve the effectiveness of the speech medium . . . to better our training techniques."

AT&T took a major step in this direction by developing a nationwide Bell System speaker-training program and a *Speaker's Manual*.

Similar steps have been taken by leading business organizations, as revealed in studies by the authors as early as 1949 and in a more recent survey by Mark L. Knapp at The Pennsylvania State University and reported in the *Wall Street Journal*. Among the many conclusions reached in this study of the 750 largest corporations in the United States is that businessmen take their speaking seriously and yet many feel that "public speaking is agonizing" for them. Some try to dodge the responsibility but most realize that through training they can be effective speakers. The *Journal* continues:

A man who is now the president of a medium-sized steel producer admits he actually turned down the job when it was first offered to him because, among other things, "I didn't feel I had the capability of speaking before a group." When he finally was prevailed upon to take the post he did so only with the "understanding that I wouldn't have to make speeches." After a while, however, he decided to take a speaking course, and eventually made his speaking debut before the New York Society of Security Analysts.

"Since I got up enough courage to make that first speech, I haven't turned down any invitations," he says. "But I still get the flutters."

But as we hope to show you, communicating is far more than an occasional Rotary speech, business lecture, or executive function. It's part of your life, and it's what helps bring us closer to other human beings. It keeps us involved and stimulates us in a way that little else can.

By personal interaction you'll find out more about yourself and what makes *you* interesting to othes. Why, you might even be asked to make a speech.

Your goals as a speaker

You've just been called and asked to give a talk at next month's Lion's Club dinner. The program chairman said your "deep convictions about slum clearance would be of great interest to the club members." Or perhaps you were invited because you have just returned from an unusual trip and the chairman wants you to speak about it. There are many *reasons for being sought out as a speaker,* centered around the kind of person you are and the ideas you generate:

1. You are active in a particular group.
2. You are an outspoken member of your corporation or business.
3. You hold a position of authority, whether at work or in the community.
4. You are reputed to be interesting and think quickly on your feet.
5. You have deep convictions and want to persuade others.
6. You have specific knowledge and abilities about which your audience wants to learn.

All these reasons are a positive endorsement of you as an individual, and being aware of them will add to your confidence and ability to organize your ideas into an interesting, well-planned talk; enable you to contribute positively in a panel or committee; or hold up your side of a two-person conversation.

We're devoting the rest of this book to the goal of helping you become a more effective communicator: understanding how the process works, selecting a subject and purpose, planning and organizing what you'll say, and supporting your ideas, persuading and motivating, practice and delivery, listening, handling special occasions, and informal communication.

The lecture circuit

Through practice, exposure, and such elements as position, publicity, and reputation, many speakers find themselves—whether intentionally or quite by accident—on what's known as the lecture circuit. You may be an author, television personality, head of a corporation, or by pursuing a personal interest like cooking, you may have achieved a reputation which puts you in demand for lecturing.

The International Platform Association, whose membership chiefly comprises professional lecturers and others who speak for a fee, symbolizes the tremendous part that speeches and lectures play in American life. A conservative estimate is that there are over 350,000 paid lectures-speeches in the U.S. a year, with this number growing every day.

In addition to augmenting his income, the lecturer gets to visit different parts of the country, meet new people, eat regional cooking, and have the satisfaction of communicating *his* knowledge and beliefs to others. There is no magic formula for being a lecturer. Just make yourself a good speaker and you may very well end up on the lecture circuit.

II

WHAT KIND OF SPEAKER
DO YOU WANT TO BE?

You don't want to become a good speaker just so others will
say "He's a good speaker," but rather so that you will be an
effective person: an effective salesman, lawyer, manager,
club member, or whatever is your aspiration.

—*Robert T. Oliver*

Have you given much thought to what kind of speaker you want
to be? Or what speaking really is? Or what a speech really is?
We realize that your ready answer to the title of this chapter
is that you want to be a *good* speaker. Then the real question
is what is meant by "good speaker" and particularly what you
mean when you have this goal.

We can go back to Quintilian, an educator in ancient Rome,
who described the good speaker as first a good man—then
skilled in speech. He believed it was more important to develop
one's self as a totally good person in order to be a good speaker,
than it was to develop the use of mere technique or external
polish. Aristotle, perhaps the greatest speech scholar and writer
of all time, advanced the dogma that the *ethos* or ethics of
the man are primary assets (or liabilities) to his effectiveness
as a speaker. Involved are the speaker's total background,
reputation, professional competence, moral conduct, and any
other factors that would influence his listeners' attitudes toward
him as they listen to what he says. These may be philosophical
concepts too hard to pin down to specific speech methods and
techniques, but they have been restated and studied in various
forms through the ages and are the basis of modern communication theory.

When Herbert Marshall McLuhan, one of the most enigmatic writers of today, advances the theory that "the medium is the message," he infers that the source and method are more important than the message itself, and in extending this belief to the speech process, we can say that the medium is *you,* the speaker. In this same light, Ralph Waldo Emerson said, "What you are stands over you and shouts so loud I cannot hear what you say to the contrary."

Interestingly, these sources all say about the same thing and are not defining the good speaker as an actor, performer, or orator. And they are not describing him as one who simply follows a set of mechanical rules or techniques or merely displays his external characteristics. There are many sound principles, methods, and techniques for the good speaker to learn and to follow. That's what this book is about. But the good speaker (and the good speech) comes more from within the man.

Self, role, and image

In terms of your immediate impact on listeners, the self that you are reaches them through your role and image. When we realize how our role changes from what we represent in the home (as father, husband, brother, sister), in business (as owner, manager, engineer, worker, clerk), and in our social environment (as friend, companion, group member, neighbor) as we pursue our daily lives, it should be obvious that we have no fixed role and that we must adjust constantly. Everyone functions in many different relationships, groups, and environments, any or all of which might form the setting for a particular speaking situation and thus call for changing degrees of authority, permissiveness, status relations, and other influences on behavior. So we tend to choose our role based on how *we* conceive it and then "present" ourselves as we feel the role demands.

But even while doing this we must realize that the listener perceives our role from *his* frame of reference, not from ours, and he interprets it as a certain *image*—the way we appear to be to him. And his image of us may be quite different from what we think it should be. Even the speaker perceives himself in a number of different images, such as being regarded by his wife as kind and gentle, by his boss as efficient and responsible, and by his friends as relaxed and cordial. Of course, many of these may be more hopeful than real, and this is one of the problems we all have in trying to assess and then live up to the kind of person we decide we are or want to be.

All of this adds up to a considerable degree of complexity in answering the title question of this chapter. We are trying to point out that one should give considerable thought to the kind of speaker he wants to be and at the same time be aware that his effort may be differently interpreted by the listener, depending on such factors as personality, setting, environment, manner, and attitude more than on speech technique alone.

What about charisma?

Charisma, a magical-sounding word of Greek origin, was used considerably during the 1968 presidential campaign as one method of assessing the qualities and characteristics of public-figure speakers. The New York *Times* addressed itself to such an analysis during the height of the presidential campaign on August 4, 1968, under the headline, "The Greeks Had a Word For It. . . ." The *Times* had considerable difficulty defining the term, which includes everything from "divine, magical, superhuman, charm, beauty, grace," to the more specific qualities of "leadership, rapport, empathy, and adaptation to other people." The article stated that certain public figures were thought to have charisma: Charles de Gaulle, Martin Luther King, George Wallace, Fidel Castro (in his early days), Gamal Nasser, the Kennedys (all of them), Franklin Roosevelt, Nelson Rockefeller, Winston Churchill, Moshe Dayan; and certain others were thought not to have it: Richard Nixon, Georges Pompidou, Ralph Abernathy, Lester Maddox, Fidel Castro (today), Shirley Temple Black, Kosygin, Confucius.

Charisma as a label can be confusing. On the one hand it relates the personal value of a speaker to his effectiveness upon others, but at the same time falsely implies that we either have certain necessary qualities or we don't. This implication includes one of the major misconceptions about speaking ability—that speakers are born and not made. Of course if one has a colorful personality, a natural liking to be with and to talk with others, a good or pleasing voice, and an enthusiastic manner, he may have an easier time as a speaker, and he may be more effective. But he may also rely too readily on this natural equipment and neglect to prepare a sound message or properly analyze his audience. Listeners may say that he is a good speaker, but others will add, "Perhaps, but what did he say?"

The record is full of endless examples of men and women who worked hard to achieve their effectiveness as speakers, neither believing the myth that good speakers are born, nor hiding behind it as an excuse for not being more effective. From Demosthenes in ancient Greece to Franklin Roosevelt, Adlai Stevenson, Clarence Randall, Dwight and Milton Eisenhower, John F. Kennedy, Richard Nixon, and Hubert Humphrey, all have attested to the long and constant effort they have made to develop their speaking ability.

So don't be too concerned about whether you have charisma.

You may have much more potential as a speaker than those who delude themselves into thinking that a "gift of gab" is all it takes.

What good speaking is not

Not mere external mechanics: Good speaking comes from within and is dependent upon self, role, image, what you are as a person, and the way you are regarded by the listener. It is not a "bag of tricks"—there are sound principles and techniques to be used.

Not something you're born with: Most good speakers have had to work hard to develop their ability. Obviously, it helps if they were born with certain basic qualities, or if these were developed as part of their personality. But everyone has the potential to be a good speaker.

Not merely personality or charisma: Whatever its value, it would be dangerous to rely on charisma alone.

Not oratory: A speech is not an oration, especially not in today's world, though it had its place a century or so ago. A few years ago, Max Eastman, well-known humorist turned speech expert, deplored "The Lost Art of Oratory." He complained that America no longer had the orators of the eighteenth and nineteenth centuries, that today's speakers lacked oratorical ability, and that thus the quality of present-day speaking was low. He longed for the Patrick Henrys, Daniel Websters, and William Jennings Bryans of the past, the orators with booming voice, dramatic display, and exaggerated gesture.

There was a place for this kind of speaking in the old days of uninformed audiences who regarded the speaker as their chief source of information and opinion and actually wanted him to talk down to them. The settings were outdoors, before large audiences, and the speech was a special event.

This is not today's audience. What Max Eastman failed to recognize is a fundamental difference in today's society—audiences are informed, sophisticated, and have access to all the mass media. They want to feel that a speaker respects this knowledge and is there to *talk things over* with them rather than to preach to them.

Not a performance: A speaker is never acting a part. Nor should he appear as though he is by his manner, gesture, and action. He is always himself and his role is himself. When members of an audience sense that its speaker is not being honest, they may lose respect for him and cease to take his remarks seriously.

Not fashioned toward a universal model: There is no such thing as the perfect speaker, one who does everything the way you would like to do it. You may like a speaker well enough to adopt some of his methods or techniques. But do not try to cast yourself in his image. Build and develop on yourself, using your own qualities to advantage and avoiding mannerisms or habits that are not effective.

Not a reading: A speech is not simply a series of words thrown at your audiences in a monotone, without expression or gesture or animation. It is not read from a printed page from which the eyes are rarely raised. This is not to say that a manuscript should never be used. But if a speech is to be read, it must be read well, as a communication with your audience.

When Alben W. Barkley was senator from Kentucky, he had this to say about reading a speech in starting to address a public gathering, "I want to say at the outset that my remarks are entirely extemporaneous. I haven't had time to reduce these remarks to a manuscript, and I do not like to read a speech anyway. I read one once, and afterward I was the guest of the host who had invited me, so I asked him what he thought of my speech. 'Well,' he said, 'I have three criticisms to make. First, you read it; second, you read it poorly; and third, it was not worth reading.'"

Not elocution: In the old days when a speech was thought of as a dramatic performance, the chief emphasis on developing speaking ability was on the refinement of posture, gesture, voice, and diction. All of these are necessary to good speech. But their useful effectiveness comes from inner enthusiasm and desire to communicate, not from mere mechanical exercise.

Not one-way transmittal: Speech is communication which must be two-way, interacting, and constantly adapted to listener reaction and feedback.

Should you have nervous energy?

Definitely yes. Nervous energy plays a key part in your effectiveness as a speaker. There are so many misconceptions about this phenomenon that we are giving it a separate heading, though it surely belongs in the list we have just developed. Many people incorrectly think that if they practice speaking and speak more often they will no longer experience any nervous feeling beforehand. Ask any good speaker, actor, or athlete who has years of experience whether he feels nervous energy building up as he approaches a new situation. Undoubtedly he does. The better he is, the more he will tell you of the part that nervous energy plays in his success.

One famous actress put it this way, after thirty-five years on the stage, "If I ever approach a performance (acting *is* a performance) without feeling nervous, I will retire immediately."

Adlai Stevenson, commenting on a major speech he was about to make as a senior at Princeton, said, "I was scared to death before I spoke. I still am, for that matter." Wayne Morse, who holds the record for the longest uninterrupted speech in Congress, has said that "Public speaking has never been easy for me." And Harry Truman similarly said, "No, I would not say that it came easily and without nervous concern."

Or watch a famous athlete before a big race or game. The better he is, the more he has tuned his mind and body to be at its best at the point when he needs it. A John Thomas in the high jump, Bob Seagren in the pole vault, Ralph Boston in the broad jump, Jim Ryun in the mile run, will spend seconds and minutes harnessing control of their nervous energy before the contest begins.

It is perfectly normal and essential that you feel some nervousness before any important social challenge. It does not take a speech to bring this about. It can be a meeting with a friend, a telephone call, an interview, or a match on the golf course. In the speaking situation, there is even more reason to make use of the nervous energy that you build up. A speech is perhaps the maximum achievement of man in that it makes use of his total ability as a person—his reasoning and intellectual process as well as his feelings.

The chief answer to the positive use of nervous energy is control, which is discussed more fully in Chapter IX.

The goal: extemporaneous speaking

Extemporaneous—a word with a great deal of meaning—does *not* mean unprepared. Speaking extempore is *natural conversational speaking, based on sound and thorough preparation.* It has been said of Harry Truman, for example, that he was not effective as a prepared speaker but when called upon to make a few unprepared remarks "extemporaneously" he was extremely effective, warm, direct, enthusiastic, and close to his listener's interests and mood. But he was speaking *impromptu*, this being the correct label for an unprepared speech.

Actually extemporaneous speaking tries to retain all the attributes of impromptu, informal speaking, as one has them in conversation—whether talking with a group of ten or a thousand—without, of course, the probable weaknesses of lack of purpose, coherence, and organization—the case with much conversation and unprepared speech. The late Eric Johnston, former president of the Chamber of Commerce of the United States, himself a speaker with rare charm and personal effectiveness, summed it up this way, "A speech is conversing with your audience as though you were in individual conversation with each member privately." A speech can thus be called *enlarged conversation*.

At the turn of the century, books devoted to the subject of speech training and development almost universally were devoted to elocution, declamation, voice and manner, and the total speech as a dramatic performance. Perhaps the first book to appear in print in the twentieth century to turn away from elocution and set forth the natural and practical methods of extemporaneous speech was by John Henry Frizzell, founder and former head of the Department of Speech at The Pennsylvania State University. In his *Notes on Public Speaking*, published in 1905, he says, "The intention is not to make orators or elocutionists. . . . They would be as out of place before an advisory board of engineers as was the familiar 'bull in the china shop.' The aim is to help each student become a plain, practical business speaker . . . to familiarize him with the method and manner of public speech, and to help him to acquire the ability to stand on his feet without awkwardness, to think as he stands, and to say plainly and clearly and with power what he thinks."

The important emphasis of this early statement is that a speech is *thinking on your feet*. And the fact that a thought process not only must be used and controlled but also revealed and communicated to the listeners makes speaking to a group a challenge. Actually, because he is alone, a speaker may have more license to develop nervous concern than the actor or athlete. The actor has the support of others on the stage, and the athlete has his teammates. The actor has chiefly to remember the lines he is to say, and the athlete has no thought process to communicate. He also has the opportunity to release nervous energy at the outset through physical activity.

The extemporaneous speaker goes through a systematic series of steps in preparing his speech, usually short of actually writing out a manuscript. He should consider his listeners first, and gather all source materials for his topic based on the audience, purpose, and occasion. Organizing his thoughts, determining his main and subpoints, and making an outline come next, followed by selection of materials for interest, support, and proof. All the while the speaker should be thinking about what will best motivate his listener. Preparation of a good set of notes and practice to insure natural, sincere delivery help the speaker's goal to communicate with the audience. All steps are discussed in detail in subsequent chapters.

Once you have developed the habit of extempore speech preparation and delivery, you will find yourself using the method even without giving conscious thought to it in all your speaking. Your *impromptu* remarks, when called on to "say a few words" at a gathering or when participating as a conference member, will tend to have more purpose, more organization, and more significant development; and your conversation will be more meaningful.

How good are today's speakers?

All of us have observed prominent public and business figures as speakers and probably have made some conclusions about their methods, manner, image, and ability. We may even pick out one or two as good or superior to others and decide that we would like to speak as they do. If you took time to list your preference as the ten best speakers in today's public scene, or in recent times, the chances are that those high on your list are the ones who really communicated with you when you saw them in person or on television. There is no question that the mass media has made us much more conscious of good and bad speaking and has afforded endless opportunity to evalute.

Franklin Roosevelt was the first prominent American to bring about this awareness. His famous "fireside chats" exuded the kind of informal close relationship with his audience that FDR wanted to achieve. Although we could not see him as he spoke on radio, his image was always present in our minds while his rich friendly voice came from what we could feel as a deeply sincere manner.

We find it much more difficult to analyze Richard Nixon as a speaker. Perhaps this is because he is not consistent in his method of speech presentation or manner. He is a rare combination of the formal, prepared, analytical with the attempt to be informal and friendly. He does not read a speech manuscript in a way to communicate warmth and close rapport with his listeners. When he speaks informally, such as at press conferences or during a campaign, he is much more effective. But even here, his sometimes labored informality seems to allow the more formal and technique-minded manner to come through. President Nixon has the unusual ability to think analytically and to have this analysis come through in difficult speaking situations. He has chosen to speak standing, without a lectern or speaker's stand in front of him (this usually gives some element of support and confidence to a speaker), and without notes in major public television settings and is able to maintain an outstanding degree of fluency and direct communication with listeners. One can see that he has done considerable extemporaneous preparation for the speaking he does without a manuscript. However, he is sometimes overly concerned about his appearance, and even his frequently slick hair tends to contribute to a more formal image than he probably wants his listeners to have. Overall, his speaking sometimes comes through as more of a performance than communication.

Lyndon Johnson changed his style of speaking so much in his public career that it is hard to analyze him as a speaker with any consistency. Before he became President, he was an animated, forceful, direct, strong speaker—excellent in those extemporaneous situations when he chose to be informal and close to his audience.

President Johnson's speaking manner was usually slow, labored, and not too effective, particularly when reading from a manuscript. The New York *Times* spoke of his "laboring" attempt to communicate: "He tries every combination. He rehearses many of his public performances. . . ." Perhaps the very fact that President Johnson's speeches were regarded as performances that had to be rehearsed are cues to his difficulties. He regained his effectiveness on those rare informal occasions when, as a Philadelphia *Inquirer* headline writer put it, "Johnson pulls out all stops in televised razzle dazzle." Said the *Inquirer* reporter on the scene, "Dropping his formal manner and his inhibitions, he addressed his East Room audience in the White House and the Nation with almost the same mannerisms and language he uses in private intimate conversation. It was a bombastic, jaunty, self-assured leader. The President also dropped the protection of his lectern—a piece of furniture for which he has such great love that it travels all over the world with him—and stepped out to meet his audience."

Hubert Humphrey probably exemplifies the natural, animated, warm, direct, conversational speaking manner that best characterizes the extemporaneous method. Even when reading from manuscript he seems to remain his natural self desiring to communicate thoughts and ideas to listeners rather than read words from a printed page as a performance. He is extremely able as an impromptu speaker, calling upon a rare ability of fluency of thought and language with minimum use of the "uh" and "er" that frequently plagues the impromptu (and sometimes the extemporaneous) speaker. His running mate in the 1968 campaign, Edmund Muskie, achieved great rapport with the American people by his candid, direct, natural manner, rarely seeming to be formal or "on stage." He made listeners feel as though he was conversing with each of them. In this important test of communicative effectiveness, the Humphrey-Muskie ticket was able to gain considerable popular support over the Nixon-Agnew effort and might have won the election if this were the only factor influencing voters.

So much has been written about the Kennedys as speakers that we can add little in this brief analysis of recent public figures. There is no doubt that their image was and is a strong factor in accounting for their success and their effectivness with audiences. Their personal charm and appearance contributes greatly. Perhaps they have been the chief motive for writers using the word charisma to try to describe these qualities in speakers. Both John and Robert Kennedy gave much evidence in their speaking of their extremely sensitive natures which contributed to their nervousness and, at the same time, to their great compassion for their audiences. This quality also gave them the great depth of inner feeling that made them the forceful, driving speakers they were. And their listeners, the

American people, always received and reacted to this feeling by their responses which were generated because they knew that the speaker had an intense desire from within to communicate his thoughts and feelings to others. Edward Kennedy carries on these qualities with similar intensity and compassion, although he seems to be a more sober and at times less forceful speaker than his brothers. He reads well from manuscript, and he combines this ability with excellent fluency in extemporaneous speaking. In this quality, he excels Robert, who had a somewhat faltering and hesitant manner in groping for thoughts and words in the extempore or impromptu situation.

There are many other public and business figures in contemporary life who could be included in this analysis. Perhaps the chief point to be made is that there is surely no one mold, style, or manner that makes today's good speaker. Each is an individual, and if he has achieved high status in public life, he has worked hard to develop his ability, and he has realized the important part his speaking plays in achieving success.

What do you conclude?

Of course you want to be an *effective* speaker—and you don't want to be necessarily like any other speaker, even though you can profit greatly by analyzing others, noting their assets and their faults, and trying to apply the principles and techniques you are learning in a better way than they do. Resolve not to rely simply on your own natural ability, but use it to build upon while retaining natural conversational qualities as a public speaker, conference member, or in any communicative situation.

2

What's Involved in Making Speeches?

III. PREPARING SYSTEMATICALLY

IV. UNDERSTANDING THE HUMAN
COMMUNICATION PROCESS

III

PREPARING SYSTEMATICALLY

> Looking back on the years, I think I have composed more
> speeches walking around, going to bed, getting up, or some-
> times by flashes in the night, than at my desk.
>
> —*Norman Thomas*

Making a speech requires preparation which pays off in pro-
portion to your effort. Once in a great while an effective speech
results from what appears to be little or no preparation—
spurred on by the excitement or challenge of a situation—
and often in today's society of mass meetings and protest settings, speakers arise with great enthusiasm to hold the attention
of their listeners. But while such a speech may have enthusiastic
delivery, coming as it does from the deep inner feelings and
beliefs of the speaker, it may lack clear purpose or coherent
organization in content.

There are classic and modern examples to illustrate the importance of preparation. Perhaps the most dramatic is Demosthenes speaking with a mouthful of pebbles before the roar of
the ocean's waves to improve his projection and to correct
a speech defect in articulation. Daniel Webster, regarded by
many as America's most consummate speaker of the nineteenth
century, made his famous "Reply to Hayne" speech (in defense
of a strong national government) in the U. S. Senate immediately
after Hayne finished speaking. His colleagues congratulated him,
calling it his finest speech, but they were amazed that he could
do this with no apparent preparation. Webster's comment was,
"Gentlemen, I have been preparing this speech all my life."
William Jennings Bryan was a poor speaker when he entered
college, but he would go out to an open field, find a tree

stump, and practice his speeches standing in the middle of a cow pasture.

Milton Eisenhower insists that he will not make a speech until he feels satisfied that he knows more about his subject than anyone in his audience. He obviously places great weight on speech content in his preparation. Hubert Humphrey, stressing the need for careful preparation, points out the most important components in a speech are a full understanding and knowledge of the subject, thorough understanding of the audience, and a deep belief in what you are saying.

Speakers will argue on whether *content* or *delivery* is more important to a good speech, but it is idle to try making a choice. A good speech is a combination of WHAT you say and HOW you say it, in relation to specific listeners. Whatever the content and delivery the total speech must be a blend of speaker, occasion, and subject.

As for the process of speech preparation, the actual sequence one goes through is to first deal with purpose and content, then to practice delivery, then to reach best mental attitude at the time the speech is given. But the attitude toward giving the speech starts to develop from the moment the speaker accepts an invitation or knows that some occasion will call for him to speak. And this attitude pervades the entire time span of preparation, even when sitting at a desk reading material about the subject or making an outline. The major areas of preparation fall into three categories:

Preparation of Self: Mental Attitude
Preparation of Speech Content
Preparation for Delivery

Preparation of self: mental attitude

Although it is easy to be indifferent toward a speech, a ho-hum feeling of the lack of importance of the situation, a conclusion that it means little or nothing to you personally, or an air of cockiness that you can "take this in stride" can all lead to disaster.

A speech is definitely a social and, sometimes, professional or business challenge. We use the word social in the sense that the speaker is in the center of a group of his peers who are looking to him to communicate something worthwhile. Regardless of whether his reason for being there is to inform them, influence them, or entertain them, it should be obvious that they will think more or less of him depending on how well he accomplishes what he sets out to do. There is no such thing as "no effect" when you confront your audience. So anyone who desires ever-increasing regard from his peers should realize that making a speech is an opportunity to build positively on his social and business relations. If he accepts this challenge and looks forward to the experience as a live, rewarding opportunity, his attitude could be worth more than much of his actual preparation of the speech itself.

Preparing yourself to speak is a combination of working out the speech content, developing a positive attitude toward wanting to speak, and harnessing nervous energy and total mental resources to be able to use them to maximum advantage. It is not unlike the athlete who conditions himself physically, learns and practices the methods and techniques needed for his particular sport, and then builds toward the kind of confident mental attitude that keys his nervous energy to the highest possible sense of achievement. For the athlete, his desire is to excel, to win, to help his team. For the speaker, his desire is to accomplish maximum communicative effect, drawing the greatest understanding, attention, and interest from his listeners.

A novice speaker can learn much from Jim Ryun. At the peak of his success as a runner, Ryun was acclaimed as the finest athlete in any sport. He approached a mile race with the epitome of physical fitness and, more important, a high pitch of mental and psychological readiness. In 1969 he lost several important races, following his defeat in the 1968 Olympics. He analyzed his problem not as lack of physical preparation but as chiefly the difficulty he was experiencing in approaching a race with the positive attitude he knew he would need to win. In 1971, his return to running indicates again a mastery of mental and physical preparation.

Preparation steps

Desire to do well is probably the initial and major stimulus to induce the right kind of mental attitude and, in turn, the best results in accomplishing any endeavor. In addition, several other factors should be considered.

Control of nervous energy. We've already agreed that it's good for you to feel your nervous energy building up as you approach the situation in which you want to be successful. But to avoid adverse effects which come from lack of preparation, you should make every effort to be well prepared. The following suggestions help contribute toward this end.

Confidence. The more you know about your subject, the more precise your purpose, the more carefully you select and organize ideas and support material and feel you know what you want to say, the more confident you will be about your speech. Reaching a proper level of confidence is probably the goal of good preparation in a total sense, for each step accomplished builds upon this objective.

Timing and spreading preparation. There are no quick formulas or short cuts to speech preparation. Neither is there an exact amount of time required for all speeches, all occasions, or all people. Obviously, time would depend on many factors, including the nature and importance of the subject, how much the speaker already knows about it, the occasion and audience, the speaker's ability to organize in his mind the way he wants to approach the speech, the degree of confidence he already has in handling this speech with this audience, and to what extent he feels he should practice his delivery. Regardless of what is needed, the following suggestions will make preparation more effective.

1. *Start to prepare early.* Most of us have a natural tendency to put things off, postponing preparation until the deadline is almost upon us. We can get away with this in many situations, but it is best not to try when preparing a speech. For a speech is something that must gradually grow on you and become a part of your thinking and feelings. Unlike a piece of written prose which is completed once it is written, a speech is not completed until it is given.

As soon as you know you will be making a speech, start thinking about it in terms of the subject and purpose, the occasion and audience, and the materials you might use. You do not necessarily need to sit down at a desk to do this. Think about the speech as you ride to work, walk around, or talk with friends.

It is a mistaken notion that the longer a speech is the more time it takes to prepare. Actually, it takes more time to prepare a short speech than a long one. Woodrow Wilson's explanation, when he was asked by a program chairman if he would make a speech and how much notice he would need in advance of the date, is significant. "If you want me to make a ten-minute speech," said Wilson, "I'd like two weeks time to prepare. If you will allow me thirty minutes for the speech, I can prepare it in a week. If you merely want me to come over and talk for an hour or two, just call me up five minutes before the dinner."

2. *Spread preparation over the full time available.* Let's assume that the average time you have from the date you know you will be giving a speech until the date it is scheduled is at

least two weeks. It is usually much longer, but don't wait for the two-week point to start preparation, for this is a good period of time in which to accomplish the above objectives as well as the specific physical steps in the process.

We can also assume that the average speech today is about twenty minutes long, although it is hard to generalize. You cannot plan the exact total time required to prepare the speech, but you can make an approximate estimate. If your total comes out to twenty hours, it is better to spend a small part of each day for fourteen days than to squeeze all preparation into the two or three days immediately before the speech. You will probably make a better speech if you start preparing early and do a little each day, even though this adds up to only ten or fifteen hours, than spending twice as much time just a few days before. Spreading the time out allows the speech to become a part of you, giving you added confidence and allowing you to develop a continuous "saturation" of the ideas you want to communicate.

Preparation of speech content

The first concern in the actual preparation of content is to *plan* what is to take place, including analysis of listeners and occasion, subject selection, source materials, and the exact purpose of the speech. Then the speaker must *organize* his thoughts and ideas, determine his main and subpoints, and make an outline. Having built the structure of the speech, he now *develops* and supports it with the best material for support, proof, and interest. Now he is ready to practice and to devise a set of notes so that he can best *communicate* it to others. While doing all this, he is concerned with the *motivation* of his listeners in order to build and develop the most effective content and delivery that will hold the attention and interest of the audience and move them in the direction of the speaker's purpose.

The steps in preparing a speech are summarized in the following table, which also indicates the chapters where each is discussed more fully.

Steps in Preparing a Speech

(THE EXTEMPORE PROCESS)

Steps	CONTENT: *What You Say*	*Chapter*
1. PLANNING	Analyzing the occasion and audience Selecting the subject Determining the exact purpose Research and gathering material	V
2. ORGANIZING	Arriving at main ideas or points Arranging in best order: the Body Making an outline Planning Introduction and Conclusion	VI
3. DEVELOPING	Selecting development and support tools and methods Considering use of visual aids	VII
4. MOTIVATING	Appealing to listener motives and interests	VIII
	DELIVERY: *How You Say It*	
5. COMMUNICATING	Practicing and presenting Using notes Controlling nervous system	IX

Preparation for delivery

Of all the steps and phases of speech planning, preparation for delivery most defies exact rules or suggestions that would be equally applicable to all speakers and situations. In an unusual case, a speaker may be ready to make the speech as soon as he has organized his ideas and thoughts. The same speaker in another instance may spend hours practicing. Again, some persons with unusual language facility may want to practice very little, especially when familiar with their subject. Others will feel more comfortable if they have gone over the speech many times in advance.

The chief objective of preparing to communicate a speech is to do so in a way that will best insure a natural, conversational manner. Keep in mind that a good speech retains these qualities of *oral style and language:*

Shorter, simpler sentences

Less complex paragraph development

Occasional broken sentences

Shorter, more colorful words

More personal pronouns ("we," "us," "you," "ours" more than "I")

More informal, colloquial words

More word contractions

More use of questions

More repetition

Sharper transitions

More internal and other summaries

More flexibility

More adaptations to specific audience

IV

UNDERSTANDING THE HUMAN COMMUNICATION PROCESS

I know you believe you understand what you think I said, but I am not sure you realize that what you heard is not really what I meant.

—*Anonymous*

It is probably more important to understand the nature of human communication than it is to use good principles and techniques in trying to achieve effectiveness as a speaker. Speaking is warm human interaction. And it is well for any student of speech to understand the process of human communication *before* he sets out to execute the specific steps in speech preparation.

Factors influencing effectiveness

We have suggested that many factors influence the success of any given speech. It might do well to summarize them here.

1. *The kind of person you are.* All the characteristics of an individual, especially the image he presents to his listeners, influence speaking effectiveness. Attitude, compassion, interest in others, enthusiasm, sincerity, and the physical indications of wanting to communicate will all play a part. So will the background, reputation, education, and general regard held by the particular listeners for the speaker.

2. *The setting and occasion.* Not only the obvious factors such as seating arrangement, comfort, light, and heating; but the nature of the event, its relative importance, and the role of

the speaker affect the outcome. If it is given in an organization or business setting, the policies and climate that have been developed over a period of time form a part of the setting against which the speech will be interpreted.

3. *The listeners.* All their personal characteristics—age, education, present knowledge, interest and attitude toward the speaker—should be acknowledged by him. The degree to which the speaker adapts to his audience and makes them feel he wants to communicate with them is the most vital factor.

4. *Barriers and their resolution.* One must first realize that there are barriers in any communicative process. Try to understand them, be aware of those most operative in the given situation, and then attempt to resolve them in your preparation.

5. *Understanding the process of human communications.* When one fully understands what is involved in his attempt to communicate with others and keeps this understanding in view at all times, he is bound to be a more effective speaker, a more compassionate person. He will have more concern for his listeners, more desire to resolve barriers, and make more and better use of good speech principles and techniques.

6. *Use of good principles and techniques.* These include all the theories and methods making up the field of speech; in short, everything one does in preparing and presenting a good speech. But simply to practice principles is not enough, and it would be a mistake to start being a better speaker by simply learning and using a set of rules.

It is interesting to note that through history many concepts and theories of speech effectiveness have evolved, depending somewhat on the social and political aspects of the times. From theory have evolved certain principles which make up the body of knowledge of speech. Then have come methods to be used in applying the principles, after which we think of techniques, which are the more precise rules to follow. The good student of speech will understand the theory behind the techniques he uses, and again, this is part of the philosophy of this book.

An example of technique derived from theory is the use of gesture for emphasis. For mere technique, the speaker raises his arm and points or pounds his fist on the table. But the theory of gesture is that the speaker, to be effective, must show his listeners the enthusiasm and sincerity he feels from within. Exactly how he makes the gesture (technique) is much less important than the fact that his feeling is genuine.

The theory behind an opening statement to attract attention, to get on common ground witth the listeners, is that the audience will respond favorably to the speaker who begins by showing his desire to communicate with them. The exact content of the statement is not as important as the speaker's indication that he is concerned with his listeners.

Modern communication theory

We have learned a great deal about human communication since the writing of *The Rhetoric* by Aristotle around 350 B.C. This book, which has remained one of the leading works on the art of discourse, presents a concept emphasizing the rhetoric or composition of the speech while also stressing the importance of the speaker's character and ethics. Though some consideration was given to the audience, the speaker was more I- or self-centered, and the speech was regarded as an instrument transmitted to the listener by the speaker.

This one-way concept of speech transmittal held through the nineteenth century, with the composition conceived solely as the instrument of the speaker. Elocution and expression emerged as styles of speaking, stressing refinement of the mechanics.

This conceptual approach to a speech as a one-way sending process might be shown symbolically by this arrow:

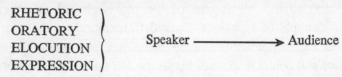

Extemporaneous speaking evolved in the early twentieth century when audiences were becoming more intelligent and informed and there was greater need to consider them in speech-making. As we have previously pointed out, this concept brought forth less formal speaking and more consideration for audience adaptation than oratory, rhetoric, and elocution. Although the concept of two-way communication was not as apparent in the early days of extempore speaking, there was a realization that the speaker had to pay more attention to audience response, place less emphasis on himself, and be more flexible in his speech delivery. This concept might be shown as follows:

EXTEMPORANEOUS
SPEAKING   } Speaker ⟵⟶ Listener

It should be noted in the above diagram that the response line of the audience runs parallel to the original transmission line of the speaker, and that they do not meet.

The modern concepts of *communication* have grown out of recent research and theory showing that the ultimate test of the speech is what the listener interprets the message to mean. The need for the speaker to be constantly aware and concerned about the feedback response from the listener is the major enlightenment of modern communication theory. We now think of a speech as communication that not only must be two-way and constantly interacting but is actually circular in nature and is a continuing circular process. To show this symbolically, as in the following diagram, requires that the feedback arrow bend toward the speaker; in turn, the continuing communicating effort of the speaker must be shown as part of the circle. Further, both the speaker who initiates the message and the listener who responds continue to get more involved in this circular process, so that the arrow meets at both ends as the circle develops. *Human communication is thus a circular process in which two or more persons endeavor to exchange meaning between them.* Unfortunately, this is not necesarily the speaker's original meaning, although his constant effort is to accomplish his communicative purpose which the major "sending" arrow represents.

Speaker ⟷ Listener

Human communication process

Perhaps the worst mistake we make as communicators is to assume that we can *send* a message into the mind and thoughts of another person. Actually, it is quite impossible for one person alone to transmit a message to another. The human communication process is you *plus* whoever is on the other end. There must be *perception* and *interpretation* by the other person. He must *want* to receive your message and will react according to the meaning it has for him.

To communicate at all, symbols must be used in some form, with words and visuals being the primary symbols. The speaker first *encodes* his message into words and actions. The listener in turn *decodes* the message and determines its meaning for him. Thus the encoding-decoding process is the crux of communicative effectiveness. And both speaker and listener must make a constant effort to resolve the many barriers that stand in the way of achieving the same meaning at both ends. The common admonition of the vexed speaker to the bewildered listener who could not understand what he said has some basis: "You're not supposed to listen to what I say; listen to what I mean."

It is also well to remember that the human communication process is always the same and does not change in formal speech, informal conversation, office interview, sales transaction, or business conference. But it does require that the communicators at both ends adapt themselves to the specific situation and to each other.

Although the circular nature of the process, the continuous flow and exchange of "sending" and "feedback," is always present with two or more communicators, each of us does a great deal of *intrapersonal communication* or communicating within the self. It happens when we sit and think, read, or watch and listen to television or a movie. We are perceiving and interpreting, learning, forming judgments, and arriving at meaning. And as we contemplate speaking to another person, the first step in the communicative act takes place within the speaker before he utters a word, as he first *perceives* that he wants to speak, *interprets* this perception and *decides* what he will say, and then proceeds to *encode* the message. Similarly, the listener will go through these same steps within himself, except that he will *decode* the message.

We can draw some general conclusions about the nature of the human communication process:

► It is not a one-way transmission.

► It is a two-way circular process that becomes dynamic and interacting.

► The objective is interpersonal, but much of the process is intrapersonal, or within each communicator.

► Both speaker and listener influence the outcome.

► Speaker and listener are likely to have different frames of reference against which they interpret meaning.

► MEANING IS PRIMARILY IN THE OTHER PERSON. It is fatal for the speaker to assume that the meaning the listener interprets (decodes) from his message will be as he wants it to be without proper adaptation to the listener's frame of reference.

Barriers to communication

There are far more barriers to effective communication than there are ways to overcome them. We tend to operate from our own frame of reference when speaking without even realizing a block exists between us and our listeners. In fact, recognizing that barriers do exist almost all the time is an essential step toward breaking them down.

What are the major barriers to communication? By looking at each one separately we can more easily understand and resolve them. Keep in mind that most barriers arise because of the different *frames of reference* of speaker and listener, since it is from his own frame of reference that each interprets meaning.

1. *"I-" or self-centered attitude.* This barrier may well include all the rest. It is quite natural to have primary concern for self and our own well-being, interests, background, experiences, beliefs, and prejudices, but this does not make for easy understanding of the other person, and it behooves us to try to project toward him and develop a YOU attitude.

A major difficulty of self-centeredness is that it increases nervousness by enhancing one's concern for accomplishing his objective. The more you- or other-person-centered the speaker can be, the better he will be able to react and adapt to his listener.

2. *Differences in background and experiences.* We don't spend all our time talking with people who live in the same community, have the same type of employment, share the same political ideas, or think alike on social issues. For this reason, one should endeavor to learn about the background and experience of his listeners before a speech. In conversation, he can question and draw out the other person to find such information. But usually much can be learned about the nature of the audience in advance of the talk.

Having done this, and having found that the audience's experiences are not the same as his in their total or general background, there can usually be found areas of common ground which both speaker and audience do share, and the message should be adapted accordingly. Again, the matter of self-centeredness looms as part of this barrier, for too often we are not willing to project toward our listener's interests and experiences, from which he has formed his frames of reference.

3. *Differences in status and position.* This is a major barrier in a work or organizational relationship where the speaker is a manager holding a superior position to the listener, or vice-versa. In social settings, the speaker's position and reputation may place him above the audience. While this can be an advantage, a boastful or arrogant manner will obviously intensify the barrier.

4. *Differences in use of feelings or logic.* This is a very subtle barrier and not readily discernible. The speaker may be trying to prove a point by what he thinks is sound reasoning, evidence, facts, and figures. Yet his listeners may be responding (if at all) only with the feeling of fear that their own lives may be in danger if the speaker's point is accepted. They really do not care about the logical proof; they want to see whether or not it could happen to them. So the logical proof of the

speaker should be tied to emotional drives and wants of the listener.

In conversing with your wife she may make a point that you doubt, and you respond by asking her, "Can you prove that?" To which her response may be to burst into tears or even leave the scene of the discussion. She was making the point out of the depths of feelings she had on this subject at this time. Proving it in the sense of logical proof was the furthest thing from her mind. The astute speaker-communicator will try to analyze the other person to ascertain whether he is speaking or listening logically or from his feelings. Conversely, he should know whether the point he is making is logical or is intended to arouse the listener's emotions.

5. *Crooked thinking*. Often our feelings, ways of reasoning, or opinions make clear thinking difficult even when an answer seems obvious. Because we have different ways of interpreting evidence or proof, it is hard to be consistent. Some of the main barriers to clear thinking are:

Inference-fact problem. Is what is being said or heard fact or inference? If it is fact—"This table is made of wood"—there should be no dispute. But if the same speaker says, "This table is made of the best substance available," he is stating an inference or value judgment.

Over generalization. This is the barrier to clear thinking that allows us to make or accept statements that claim too much. Or, in a speech to instruct or inform, we may deal with *part* of a subject, leaving out vital areas and implying to the audience that we have covered the whole subject.

Either-or problem. We are sometimes inclined to reduce a situation to just two alternatives, such as claiming that we should do either A or B, and proceeding to show that A will not work, thus leaving B as the only thing to do. Actually, there may be C and D or other solutions to the situation at hand. Or there may be variations on A or B that do not make either alternative the absolutes we claim.

Cause-effect problem. Observing some condition in society, or in a physical setting, we reason what caused it. In complex conditions, it is very difficult to reason this with any certainty. Even the cause of a headache is sometimes difficult to diagnose. Conversely, when we reason that a plan, proposal, or some specific act if put into practice will cause something to happen, we are claiming that a cause-effect relationship exists for which there may or may not be proof. Politicians are always claiming that "elect me (the cause) and you will have good times in the future (effect)." We know that in many instances this is crooked thinking at its worst. A physician may more likely reason that "if you take this medicine (cause), your headache will go away (effect)." He bases this statement on sound medical knowledge, clinical research, and past experience in establishing a causal relationship. But we should be wary of claiming too much in cause-effect reasoning. Crooked thinking or bad reasoning is discussed in detail in Chapter VIII.

6. *The setting.* The place, time, physical arrangements, nature of the occasion, kind of audience, and all the factors making up the speech situation can be the speech's biggest barriers. In addition to the obvious factors of seating arrangement, light, heat, comfort, and visibility, the mood or attitude of the audience in a particular setting may be vital. Events immediately preceding the speaking situation could generate interest or feelings which an astute speaker will recognize and include throughout his talk.

7. *Resistance to change.* The principle of "least effort" influences all of us. Despite the fact that we sometimes seek innovation or change, we tend to stick to the *status quo* as the most comfortable way of doing things. Speakers must be aware of this resistance, particularly when presenting points of view in persuasion. You should try to show why the change should be

made, the need for it in terms of present conditions, and its advantages over other methods or ways of thinking. This is a part of persuasion and motivation which we discuss later. Recognition that the barrier exists in a given situation should lead to a concern about proper attitude and degree of directness in introducing the change. A good general axiom is that the stronger the change the less directly it should be introduced, and the more evidence and proof of its values presented to the particular listeners. "Closed mindedness," or complacency about our own beliefs, is another way to characterize this barrier.

8. *Refute rather than understand.* This barrier is somewhat related to the change barrier in that it has to do with our tendency to like to argue and to disagree with another person, whether he be a formal speaker or a friend in conversation. This is a fundamental democratic privilege, but it is too quickly undertaken at the expense of understanding. Instead of listening for meaning in what is being said, we try to make up our reply and refutation before we really understand the speaker's point, and even before he has finished with it.

9. *Different speaking and listening rates.* The average rate of speaking is 125 to 140 words per minute, although we can listen at a rate of 400 to 500 words per minute. It's apparent that the listener has a great deal of time on his hands, which can facilitate the communicative process or block it. The tendency is to daydream with this extra time, letting thoughts wander away from the speaker's message. The speaker should realize that he must show sufficient enthusiasm and sincerity for the listener in his manner. He must also adapt the content, in terms of his main points, supporting material, and language to his listener's interests and background to a degree that he will want to listen actively, using his extra time to apply, interpret, and evaluate what the speaker is saying. It is impossible to speed up the rate of speaking to match the audience's

listening ability, but one should at least keep in mind that a slow, droning manner can tune out any listener.

10. *Language*. Many speakers find this the major barrier and would place it first on the list, because language is the most obvious symbol used to encode and decode communication into meaning. In placing it last, we point out that our list is not in order of importance, for there would be no way to rank the barriers. One may loom largely in a given time and place and then not be operative at all in another. Since language is merely the external symbol chosen by the communicator while some other barriers may be operative, it is a mistake to regard it as THE barrier. But it indeed causes trouble.

Words in themselves have different meanings to different people or when used in different contexts, such as "cheap," "good," "bad," "smart," "late." They also assume different meanings when put together in a sentence. And when we add the setting, the persons involved, and their relationship, it is difficult to be sure what the original communicator meant.

A supervisor asked his secretary to go to a certain room and get "the papers lying on the desk." She returned with the wrong papers. She had found two tables in the room, neither of which looked like a desk but both had papers on them. She guessed incorrectly and picked the wrong papers from the wrong "desk." If the speaker had been more specific and described the papers more fully she might have taken the right ones.

Among the many suggestions that can be offered about words and language, try to keep these in mind:

▶ Words mean different things to different people.

▶ Too many people assume that a word's meaning is universal.

▶ The literal meaning of a word is only part of the real meaning in the given situation and current frames of reference.

► Words should be adapted to the level and interest of the audience.

► Simple short words are usually better than long ones.

► Oral language qualities, such as short sentences, more repetition, more personal pronouns, and more adaptation to audience should be used.

► Technical words with unique meanings or jargon should be avoided or else explained in more common language.

► One word misinterpreted can change the entire meaning in a sentence.

3

The Substance of Your Speech

V

PLANNING THE SPEECH

On the day of the dinner of the Oyster Monger's Society, what a noble speech I thought of in the cab.
—*William Makepeace Thackeray*

In most situations planned in advance, the speaker-to-be gives considerable thought to the coming setting and his role in it. Then he approaches the more specific process of reducing this thought to decisions and action. Assuming a week or two to plan a speech, it is important to make decisions, particularly on subject and purpose, within the first few days. In less formal preparation for speaking, as in a meeting, one may gradually develop a desire to speak on a particular subject as he hears others speak and as he analyzes the group situation and occasion. He sometimes gradually, sometimes quickly, brings the four steps to bear in his planning, whether his preparation time is long-range or quite limited:

Analyzing the audience and occasion
Selecting the subject
Determining the exact purpose
Gathering material and research

Analyzing the audience and occasion

The audience and the occasion influence any speech. So you should know something about the setting, type of meeting, events surrounding the date, emotions and attitudes of the audience, and other speakers on the program. The place of the speech is also part of the occasion. It is quite different to plan a speech to be presented in the formal setting of a board room than as part of informal remarks at a PTA dinner.

If speech planning is considered in terms of communication, one can develop his ideas in answer to these questions:

What are my communication goals? This is the purpose of the speech; what you want to accomplish in terms of listener understanding, behavior, and attitudes.

What communication problems and barriers must I anticipate and resolve? This is audience analysis and the examination of the factors that might stand in the way of achieving listener meaning from the speech message.

What are the best available methods to achieve maximum communication results? This brings to mind all the principles of speech that should be employed: the clearest and most effective organization, the best use of support and proof, and other techniques that will bring the speech closest to the audience.

How can listener feedback be noted and interpreted? This is thinking beyond the speech to possible ways to measure effectiveness, determine follow-up, and other steps to be taken.

In trying to analyze your audience's characteristics, keep in mind the following:

Objective, physical, or factual information, including what you can put together to describe the audience physically (i.e., age, sex, occupation, and education). Membership in groups, politics, and similar factual knowledge, which is not always as easy to ascertain, is valuable.

Present interests. We are not as concerned about the listeners' attitudes and beliefs as we will be later, but areas and degrees of interests are important in selecting a speech topic. We look at the factual characteristics of age and education and group membership to get keys to interests. We also look at the setting, the place, the event, the time. In speaking to a Yale University audience of chiefly male students at a time of campus unrest over the Vietnam war, Mrs. Lyndon Johnson chose to speak instead on her favorite interest, beautification of America's cities. This was a case of allowing speaker interest to supersede audience interest in subject selection, and consequently, she spoke to a very apathetic audience.

The interest of the occasion gives rise to the most important speeches in history. At Richmond, Virginia, before the American Revolution, Patrick Henry's famous "Call to Arms" sounded out the audience's desire to fight the British. In more recent times, the Cuban missile crisis brought President John F. Kennedy to the microphones to talk to the world at a time when interest in self-preservation was paramount. These were moments in history when the perfect combination of occasion, speaker, and audience interest blended together so that the speaker's words were as close to audience interests as possible. Most of us do not expect such situations where our words will be the center of attention, but we want to come as close as we can in each setting.

Present attitudes, beliefs, and feelings. These are, of course, the most difficult characteristics to ascertain and are the least likely to lend themselves to objective analysis. Again, some information about the audience may give us clues as to their attitudes and beliefs. If they are all adults and have sons of draft age, they will have high interest in a speech on America's military involvements. But it may be difficult, if not impossible, to know whether they approve of the national policies or not.

We suggest using the following form to make a careful and systematic analysis of the audience and occasion for each speech. You will then have a solid foundation for proceeding with your organizing and developing steps.

AUDIENCE AND OCCASION ANALYSIS SHEET

Use this form for initial planning of the speech

Occasion

The setting:
　　Place _____
　　Date _____ Time _____
　　Sponsoring group _____
Chairman _____ Other speakers _____
Speaker _____ Subject _____
Title of speech _____ Length _____

Audience

General nature _____ Sex _____ Size ____
Background or occupations _____
Education level _____
Special factors _____

Relation to subject:
　　Present knowledge _____
　　Present interest _____
　　Ability to learn or respond _____

Relation to purpose:
　　General purpose of speech _____
　　Statement of exact purpose of speech _____
　　_____
　　Audience attitude toward speaker _____
　　Attitude toward purpose _____
　　Beliefs or feelings to consider _____

Adaptations to be made:
　　In the Introduction _____
　　In handling subject and purpose _____
　　In organizing and developing speech _____
　　Other _____

Selecting the subject

Unless a subject is given to you by the program chairman or group, or it emerges automatically from the nature of the occasion, several major factors will contribute to choosing a topic. And even when it is suggested to you, some or all of these factors have probably been considered:

The occasion
Your knowledge, interests, and beliefs
Your listeners' knowledge, interests, background, and beliefs
Your sources and availability of materials
The length of the speech

The occasion as a source of subjects has already been discussed. A business staff meeting pretty much controls the subjects that will have to be discussed at the time, and you have little choice. If some latitude does exist, it is in the area of subjects that are most timely or even urgent. In other settings, you may be asked to speak on any subject you may select. Here the variety of possibilities may delay your decision. Remember that you can't proceed with the actual preparation of the speech until you have your subject. *Don't put this off.*

Your knowledge, interests, and beliefs. Most good subjects come from within the speaker. Speech is "thinking out loud" revealing what we are and what we know, the sum total of our background, education, experiences, and beliefs. All of these are part of our daily conversations with people, and it is quite logical that they will be drawn upon for topics and materials in making speeches. The more you know about a subject and the more deeply you believe or feel what you are saying, the better you can speak about it. But you are not looking for a "ready-made" subject on which you are already fully informed. You must accept the fact that you will have to acquire more knowledge about it.

Your own mind is thus the primary reservoir for speech topics, not only in choosing a subject in which you have interest and some knowledge, but in deciding on your speech purpose and analyzing your beliefs and feelings on the issues that emerge in this subject, if your purpose is to be persuasive.

Your listeners' knowledge, interests, background, and beliefs should be given consideration. The ideal choice of subject is one that interests the speaker and audience and appropriately suits the occasion. If you have this combination, there will be fewer factors to consider in trying to develop audience interest. Given a choice between high speaker interest in a subject and high listener interest, you should opt for the former, for it is easier to motivate your listeners and develop the speech with interesting and attractive material since you can speak with more enthusiasm, conviction, and sincerity.

The length of the speech may be a major factor in choosing a subject, while considering both your own and your listeners' interests. Length is also a major factor in determining the exact purpose of the speech and the scope of the subject as you plan to handle it. Most all subjects have to be narrowed down for a particular speech. Yet, if you have just five minutes to speak, certain subjects would have to be ruled out completely as being too complex, such as an exposition on U.S. foreign policy or the latest line of computers.

Topics for speeches

In the latter part of this book, we present suggested speech topics and show how some of them might be developed. At this point we suggest that you explore your own background and interests and start making up a list of subject areas for your future use. Assume that you will be speaking to a small group, either to explain or inform or to get them to believe as you do. Don't avoid a topic because you have doubts whether you know enough about it at this point or think that an audience would not be interested. You can handle both such contingencies later. Make two lists, something like this:

Information I could communicate to others	*Beliefs and feelings on which I could influence and persuade others*
1. How watches are made (Present work)	1. Drive carefully (Was in a bad accident)
2. An automobile assembly line (Present work)	2. Values of the United Nations (Reading and observations)
3. The Grand Canyon (Took a trip)	3. Exercise for better health (Feeling of basic need)
4. Making birdhouses (Hobby)	4. Everyone should have a hobby (Experience)
5. How to play poker (Hobby)	5. The President is pursuing the best policy (Reading and convictions)
6. How to milk a cow (Raised on a farm)	6. Safe work practices on the job (Basic need experience)
7. The history of my company (Work experience)	7. It pays to be courteous (Feeling and experience)
8. The company policy on . . . (Work experience)	8. Oil is the best fuel to heat a home (Conviction and reading)
9. Growing annuals in the garden (Experience and reading)	9. Inflation must be stopped (Conviction and reading)
10. Walking down Fifth Avenue (Experience)	10. Invest in the stock market— or Do not invest in the stock market (Conviction and experience)

Determining the exact purpose

Listeners like speakers to guide them, clearly and directly, toward a response. They don't like to work to figure what you're driving at or to listen to vague and mixed up objectives. If your listener has to work too hard to follow your speech purpose and ideas, he can easily let his mind wander in other directions.

Purposive speaking means setting an exact goal and sticking to it, doing everything you can in both what you say and how you say it to accomplish this goal. It means aiming at the center of the target and hitting it.

Just what do you want to accomplish in making a speech? Every time you speak, there is some reason. In informal conversation it may not be too important, but as the situation becomes more formal your purpose assumes greater importance. If the successful accomplishment of a work assignment in your department depends on your employees understanding what they are to do, you must determine exactly what they must comprehend in giving your instructions. If your livelihood depends on persuading customers to buy or getting voters to vote, then your persuasive aim must be clear. And when you simply want to hold attention and interest and have others enjoy what you are saying, then you should know this to be your goal.

We are thus trying to arrive at the **general purposes** of speaking. Most often there are two basic goals, with a third occasional one, that of interesting and entertaining others.

To inform, instruct, and achieve understanding. A major responsibility of each of us is to pass on information or instruction to others, to a child learning to do something for the first time, to workers on the job, to a motorist who is lost and wants to learn the way. Explaining, describing, narrating, and otherwise giving information are objectives of all speaking, including persuasion. But we should know whether our purpose is one, the other, or both.

To persuade and influence. All speaking influences people in some way. When a listener understands what he has heard, he may be influenced to think or act; thus, persuasion may be accomplished by informing. But we should know when our objective is to persuade, whether directly or as an incidental product of informing. Persuasion attempts to influence attitudes, beliefs, feelings, or actions. This objective never ceases. It includes trying to persuade your wife to make something for dinner, your children to make less noise, your boss to give you a raise, and a group of people (an audience) to support a cause, vote for a candidate, or drive more carefully.

To interest, entertain, or achieve pleasant listening. This purpose is more likely to be evident in social conversation or at special speaking situations where everyone just wants enjoyment from the speaker's remarks. This is typically the after-dinner setting, although much serious speaking is done in this setting today. The average person rarely finds himself needing to "entertain" listeners in a formal speech. He will more often want to inject lightness—perhaps an anecdote—in his more serious speeches.

Your **personal purpose** in a given speech may be related to the general and exact purposes you want to accomplish with respect to your subject. But whether you want to inform or persuade on a given subject, you may have more you want to accomplish before this particular audience. You may want to make a favorable contact for some future relationship either with the group or individuals in it. There may be just one or two people in the group, such as your immediate superior or your wife, whom you particularly want to please. Factors such as these will not necessarily affect your goals and methods of preparing and presenting the speech, but they may contribute in some way to your content and manner, the inclusion or exclusion of certain material, or even the scope of your purpose.

The **exact or specific purpose** is within the broad general purpose and is the precise goal you want to accomplish with your listeners. It is one of the most important steps in speech preparation, for the entire speech is built to accomplish this end. Usually it is determined after a subject and a general purpose is established. However, we sometimes select a subject, determine the general purpose, and arrive at the exact purpose as a composite step.

Arriving at the specific purpose is essentially a narrowing process, somewhat as depicted in the diagram below. The subject is usually first thought of in a broad sense; then we decide that, of the many objectives we might try to accomplish, our major general purpose is to inform on some phase of this subject. It is in this stage that many speakers remain fuzzy and uncertain, failing to determine exactly what information they want to communicate to the audience in their *exact* purpose. Your goal should be written down as a concise, clear statement of just what you want to accomplish, just what you want your audience to know, feel, think, believe, or do when you are finished.

Arriving at the specific purpose is thus an attempt to channel the exact response wanted from the audience, as the speaker narrows his broad subject to fit this particular objective.

Speech title and exact purpose relationship. The objective of phrasing a title in attractive or figurative language should not be sought at the expense of clarity in indicating the general subject, though the title may be important for publicity and promotion. Titles do not normally indicate the exact purpose of the speech, particularly where the speaker wishes to withhold it until he is actually speaking.

Broad titles such as "The United Nations," "The Wine Country of France," and "Hobbies" indicate the probability of

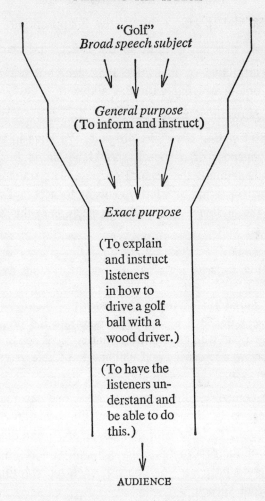

"Golf"
Broad speech subject

General purpose
(To inform and instruct)

Exact purpose

(To explain
and instruct
listeners
in how to
drive a golf
ball with a
wood driver.)

(To have the
listeners un-
derstand and
be able to do
this.)

AUDIENCE

an informative general purpose. If they are changed to read "What is the Future of the United Nations?" or "Turn your Hobby into a Career at Home," a persuasive general purpose is indicated. Here are a few suggestions for titles:

► Be brief (three to five words)

► Reveal the general subject area

► Reveal the specific subject area if appropriate

► Do not necessarily indicate the exact purpose

► Use attractive or figurative language, but not at the expense of not complying with the above

► Try phrasing it as a question

Method of stating the exact purpose. We have indicated that the exact purpose of a speech should be stated in a sentence that extends or limits the general purpose. The statement should be set down in terms of what you want to accomplish or what you want the audience to experience, such as in this example of a speech on golf:

Subject: Golf
Title: "How to Drive a Golf Ball" *or* "How's Your Driver Working?"
General Purpose: To inform and instruct
Exact Purpose: To explain and demonstrate the proper way to drive a golf ball with a driver *or* I want my audience to understand the proper way to drive a golf ball and to be able to apply this to their own game.

It is, of course, readily observable that one can make dozens of speeches, each with different exact purposes, on the general subject of golf, to inform or persuade, or to entertain. And it would be of interest to take any general subject and see how many different purposes you can list, each representing the goal of a different speech.

Here are some examples of speech subjects and purposes:

Subject: The company I work for
Title: "Our Company's History" *or* "How This Company Developed"
General purpose: To inform
Exact purpose: To inform a group of company employees about the origin, history, and recent developments of the XYZ Company *or* I want my listeners to understand and have the facts

concerning the origin, history, and recent developments of the XYZ Company.

General Subject: Automobiles
Title: "Your Next Automobile"
General Purpose: To persuade
Exact Purpose: To convince my listeners that the A automboile is the best in its field and to buy one for their next car *or* I want each of my listeners to buy the A car.

Gathering material and research

The primary source of material for your speeches lies within yourself, your experiences, background, associates and friends, and reading. You should probe your mind for points of reference that will either immediately give you some good material to use in the speech or lead you to sources of it.

The major *sources of material* should be these:

Yourself	Magazines
Your associates	Reference encyclopedias
Your friends	and almanacs
Radio and television	Books
Newspapers	

As a primary step you should make a list of your ideas and the materials you will need to develop and support. What you are looking for is, basically, facts and information in the form of data and statistics, examples and incidents, testimonials of authorities, all of which we discuss as developmental tools in Chapter VII. But do not be satisfied with superficial or inaccurate information. Here is where you may need to go to printed source materials. Again, you may find that your business or professional associates can be a source of material and ideas. Feel them out and discuss the subject with them. This will not only provide possible materials to use, but it will help you in your total job of audience analysis by giving you a closer insight into the way others think on your subject and purpose.

Once you think you have the material you need, you will want to sort, classify, and perhaps discard. Do not rest on your files. An experience or something you come across in the daily paper just before your speech may be better to use than an example you had planned to include in your initial preparation.

Build a Speech File: Make it a habit of carrying with you some blank three by five cards so that you can record anything you find in your daily experiences and reading and put in a speech file. Here are some suggestions for doing this:

► Keep in mind a general list of subject areas and jot down ideas related to these as you think of them or come upon them in talking or reading.

► Record significant or unusual facts in the form of statistics, events, and people.

► Record unusual or interesting stories or events, or anecdotes.

► Record choice quotations.

► Put only one item on each card. Then decide where the card belongs in your general subject list, or in your list of main points you intend to make for a particular speech, and put the card under such point.

VI

ORGANIZING IDEAS

Cut it in half, tighten, and get rid of the damn jokes.
—Lyndon Johnson

Listeners like speakers who communicate with them in an orderly, systematic, easy-to-follow manner. Although all listeners may not be orderly and systematic in their own thinking habits, it does not follow that they can piece together a jumbled mass of ideas from a speaker—nor will they usually make any real effort to do so. Organizing ideas in a speech and making a good outline from them is like preparing a blueprint for a new home, a requisite that few home builders would do without.

Most of us can remember the teaching we received in our English classes that lists the trilogy of *unity, coherence,* and *emphasis* as the primary rules of good discourse. We are really bringing these rules to bear again as we discuss the principles and methods of good speech organization. A speech must have a unified message throughout, as represented by the speaker's exact purpose and theme. Then the points he makes in accomplishing this purpose must fit together clearly into a coherent whole, and with proper emphasis on important ideas.

For the speaker, the time and effort he devotes to organizing his thoughts will have immeasurable value in clearing his thinking about subject and purpose. It forces him to relate the subject to his own and his listeners' thought process, and it strengthens his confidence in the assurance that he knows what points he wants to make, in what order, and with what purpose. This chapter deals with the selection of main ideas in the speech, the patterns and methods of organizing these points according to the speech purpose and the listeners, and the principles and methods for making a useful speech outline that will lead to maximum use of the extempore method of speaking. These principles are the basis of organizing the many suggested speech outlines in the latter part of the book.

Steps in organizing a speech

Good organization involves arriving at a pattern and sequence of speech ideas that will best accomplish the specific purpose of listener reaction. A series of steps should be followed in this order:

Determine the main ideas or points
Organize them into the best sequence
Break down each main point into subpoints
Plan the Conclusion
Plan the Introduction

In terms of the continuity of speech organization, this sequence suggests that the Introduction is the last step in the process. This may seem illogical, since the Introduction is, after all, delivered first. But you really cannot determine just how you want to introduce the speech and lead up to the main points in the Body until you know what you are introducing. You also want to keep the Introduction flexible up to the time of the speech presentation, for there may be last minute adaptations to the audience, the occasion, and people that you would want to incorporate.

The main ideas

In the logical progression of steps in speech preparation, it is subject selection in relation to the audience and occasion that usually occur first. These are followed by a narrowing to general and specific purpose. Next the speaker decides on the main ideas or points that will make up the substance of his speech. If the subject is suggested to the speaker or he has a definite subject and purpose in mind initially, this first step will have been accomplished. What actually happens in many situations is that the speaker goes over the many thoughts, ideas, information and knowledge, opinions, and feelings he has on different subjects, and from these the subject and purpose emerge.

Regardless of which comes first, the speaker must arrive at the main points he wants to make in his speech so that his exact purpose is accomplished. Putting this another way, the main points should be a clear-cut division of a statement of specific purpose. If we liken the purpose statement to a pie, the real question is whether one tosses it at his audience in Mack Sennett-fashion, or serves it up one slice after another, each piece representing a logical progression of ideas.

THIS?

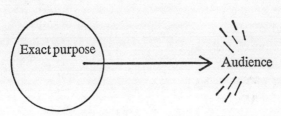

Splattering of pie (points)

OR THIS?

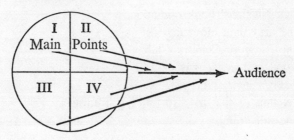

Serving up each piece (point)

The first list of ideas a speaker makes in working toward his main points is usually not a list of points alone but a mixture of major and minor ideas, facts, opinions, and examples. Many speakers mistakenly assume that this in itself is the framework of the speech. But that list is only a beginning. It must be made and remade until examples, facts, ideas, and opinions are separated from one another and from other developmental material. This is a process of *synthesis* that is essential but too frequently ignored.

For example, an informative speech on golf may have the exact purpose of instructing the listeners in the proper way to drive a ball. By first making a random list of ideas as they occur to you, the following stages may result:

1. *Make random list:*
   Grip on the club.
   Kind of club.
   Position of feet.
   Arnold Palmer.
   Start of the swing.
   Use of the eyes.
   Position of the body.
   The follow-through.
   Addressing the ball with the club.
   200 yards.
   Jack Nicklaus' book quotation.
   The arms and elbows.
   The Biltmore Country Club.
   Wood and metal drivers.
   Today's interest in golf.
   Relation of the drive to other golf strokes.
   The full swing.

2. *Group and regroup, separating points from development and support material.*

During this step, attempt should be made to start separating main points from subpoints, then gradually refining both:

Points	*Development and support*
Position of the body.	Arnold Palmer (example).
Position of feet.	Jack Nicklaus (example-testimony)
The arms and elbow.	200 yards (number).
Grip on the club.	Biltmore Country Club (example).
The full swing.	
Start of the swing.	
The follow-through.	
Addressing the ball with the club.	
Use of the eyes.	
Kind of club.	
Wood and metal drivers.	
Today's interest in golf.	
Relation of the drive to other strokes.	

3. *Continue to synthesize into 3 or 4 main points, separating Introduction and Conclusion points from these.*

The above list still shows seven ideas that appear to be main points, but this is too many; some, in fact, are subordinate points. As the actual main points emerge, subordination of subpoints and supporting material also takes place, as follows:

Today's interest in golf (Introduction, not a main point).

Should be able to drive 200 yards (Introduction).

Relation of drive to other strokes (Introduction).

Position of body in driving (main point).

Position of feet.

Use of arms and elbows.

Addressing the ball with the club.

Use of eyes.

Hands and other parts of body (new subpoint).

Gripping the club.
>   Kind of club for driving.
>   Grip A (new subpoint).
>   Grip B (new subpoint).
The full swing.
>   Start of swing.
>   Use of body, arms, wrists in the swing (new subpoint).
>   Follow-through.

4. *Rearrange the main points into best possible sequence as actual outline emerges.*

This list probably has the best number of main points. However, the sequence shows "Gripping the club" as third when it should be first to have the best time sequence and should be expanded to include "selecting" as well. In the final draft stage, as outlined below, some of the points have been revised and are stated more fully, showing the results of the constant process of refinement. Developmental material, such as examples, is shown under the appropriate subpoint.

DRAFT OF FULL SPEECH OUTLINE

Introduction

I. There is great interest in golf today.
>   A. At the Country Club in our city ———— people play daily.

II. With practice, you should drive an average of 200 yards.
>   A. The drive is basic to a good golf game.
>   B. Other strokes.

Body

I. Selecting and gripping the club.
>   A. Types of drivers.
>   B. Grip A.
>   C. Grip B.

II. Position of body.
   A. Feet and legs.
   B. Upper body and arms.
      1. Arnold Palmer positions.
III. Addressing the ball with the club.
   A. Hands and arms.
   B. Use of eyes.
IV. The full swing.
   A. Start of swing.
   B. Use of body, arms, and wrists.
      1. Jack Nicklaus method.
   C. Follow-through.

Conclusion

I. Work on these suggestions to improve your game.
   A. Summary.
   B. Future application.

RULES FOR MAIN IDEAS

We are now ready to summarize the essential factors and criteria for arriving at the main points in a speech. Consideration of the speaker, his audience, and the subject and purpose to be accomplished are all involved.

Related to yourself as speaker, consider:
   1. Your knowledge of the subject.
   2. Availability of materials for support and development.
   3. Your feelings and beliefs, in relation to persuasion.
Related to the audience:
   1. What is their present knowledge of the subject?
   2. What is their ability to understand and learn?
   3. What are their attitudes, feelings, and beliefs, in relation to persuasion?

In the actual selection and decision to use them, the main ideas should:

1. Add up to the accomplishment of the specific purpose.
2. Number about two to four.
3. Be stated clearly and for best listener reaction.
4. Be related to the time limit of the speech.
5. Be arranged for maximum effectiveness.

One of the major tests for the use of a main point in a speech is whether it helps accomplish the specific purpose. It must be *relevant* to the subject and goal of the speech.

The number of main points depends on what is needed to achieve *coherence* and maximum listener comprehension and acceptance. The speaker who guides his listeners toward clear and orderly thinking on the subject must remember that the audience may not have given any thought to organizing its own thinking on the subject beforehand. In doing this now for the first time with the speaker, listeners may be confused by too many ideas and left straining to separate the really essential points from the lesser ones—unless the speaker helps them. The audience cannot follow more than a few points: Given ten points to remember, many listeners will forget them all. The average listener, however, can retain two to four points, a rule that should be observed whether the speech is five minutes or thirty minutes in length. In the longer speech, it is probable that the speaker's specific purpose is broader and he would have one or two more main points. But not necessarily so. Most treatments of a subject and purpose can best be reduced to this number, using the principle of synthesis and subordination in finding the subpoints, and grouping and regrouping until three or four main points have emerged. In the longer speech, of course, there is also fuller treatment of each point and subpoint as well as more use of developmental material.

Patterns of speech organization

Every speech should be organized according to a pattern that best fits its purpose. The obvious divisions of Introduction, Body, and Conclusion should be observed, for every speech must have a beginning, a main development, and an ending. In terms of the major divisions of the speech, what the listener wants and what the speaker can do to fulfill these wants are:

Divisions of Speech	Listener Attitudes and Wants	What Speaker Does
INTRODUCTION	Apathetic or neutral	Gain attention Motivate interest
BODY	Understanding or agreement Involvement Proof and support Facts and specifics	Have clear main points Be well-organized Use concrete facts and other good development and support adapted to listener
CONCLUSION	Future application and usefulness	Summarize Show what to think or do

Another approach to a basic pattern of speech organization stems from what has become accepted as the *normal thought process* that all of us tend to follow in addressing our thinking to any subject or situation. The speaker must remember that all communication is an attempt to guide the thinking (and feelings) of the other person in the direction of his own thoughts and purpose. This pattern should therefore be kept in mind and adapted as may fit the speech needs.

Steps in Normal Thought Process	*Speaker's Adaptation to Pattern of Organization*
1. Attention drawn to situation, need, or problem.	Introduction arouses attention and interest by adapting subject and purpose to listener needs.
2. Consideration or analysis of situation, need, or problem.	Body of speech explains or informs, if need is to have information, or shows extent of problem and its implications to listener, usually in persuasion.
3. Look at possible solutions and weigh and analyze these.	As speaker presents information he is filling the need (or solving the problem), as in speech to inform. As he shows possible solution and values of
4. Determine best solution.	best solution he is helping the listener determine his beliefs and course of action, as in speech to persuade.
5. Take action.	Body of speech points to application for use of information or plan of action and values of this to listener, as in persuasion. Conclusion makes appeal and reinforces future action advocated.

IN SPEECHES TO INFORM

The main objective of a speech to inform is to satisfy the listener's need for information. The concern of the speaker should be to arrive at the best possible arrangement or sequence of his information, chiefly in terms of his main points in the Body of the speech. Most information falls readily into one of the following sequences.

Time or chronological. Time sequence applies to the speech on company history or in describing a baseball game, a process, or an event.

Space. This order controls when the objective is to present information on a specific place or object, such as "The City of Amsterdam," or "The Campus at Cornell." One would start at a certain geographic point and proceed from one location to another in a systematic order, gradually making up the whole.

Logical or topical. When the subject does not lend itself to either of the above, the speaker must determine how to arrange his main points in the most logical or orderly sequence. If he is chiefly describing the physical city of Amsterdam, he would use a space order. But he may want to inform about the city's government and its commercial life as main points. In this case, he would have to decide what order to use that would best hold listener attention and interest, along with other factors considered below.

Causal. When a speaker analyzes cause and effect, he should discuss first one and then the other. Such might occur in informing about laboratory research (cause) and its results (effect).

All of these possible sequences, and any other special order to best suit the subject and purpose, must be considered in relation to these factors of listener analysis:

1. What will best hold his attention and interest?
2. What must he know before he will understand the next point?
3. What will be easiest for him to understand or follow? How can one best go from easy to difficult?
4. What is best for clarity?
5. What is best for persuasion and acceptance of the speaker's specific purpose?

The primary goal in speaking to inform is *to make clear* and *achieve understanding* with the listener. These communicative desires might occur in informal conversation or social situation in a group, or in making a talk to a group, or in a more formal presentation or briefing in a business setting.

In any or all of these, we might also want to achieve motivation and persuasion, in terms of arousing interest or in suggesting future use, action, and application of the information. Thus, much informative speaking has at least a secondary goal of persuasion. Similarly, when the primary goal is persuasion, such as in selling a product or getting listeners to travel to a certain country, much of these speaking objectives will be accomplished by including a great deal of information about the product or the country.

When the primary goal is merely to hold interest and attention, or to entertain, the actual content will be largely informative, again in the form of facts, description, narration, or explanation. And perhaps many opinions and judgments will be expressed. The informative process, then, runs through all speaking and listening objectives.

IN SPEECHES TO PERSUADE

Persuasion is a much more complex process than informing. In addition to considerations of audience interest in the subject, extent of present knowledge, and the ability to learn, the persuasive speaker must consider the listener's attitude and beliefs toward the subject and purpose. Influencing these is the dominant goal of persuasion.

Since most of our attitudes grow out of a need that requires us to reason toward the desired answer, persuasive speeches tend to follow the normal thought process or some variation of it.

These speeches also involve consideration of the "stock issues" that form part of our attempt to find the best way to think or act. The relationship of our thought process to the issues is something like this:

Normal Thought Process	Stock Issues or Questions
Attention and interest.	
Problem or situation.	Is there a need (for a change or to keep the *status quo*)?
Possible solutions.	What are the ways to satisfy the need?
Best solution.	What is the best way? Is it better than any other way? Will it bring new evils (needs, problems)?
Action.	Can this be put into effect? Is it practical? Will it work?

Three major ways of handling a persuasive topic are the *problem-solution* speech; *this or nothing,* where the speaker tries to show that his solution is the only workable one; and the speech emphasizing the solution's *positive advantages* over other possible methods.

Problem-solution:

Thus the persuasive speaker tends to organize his points in this approximate sequence, or some variation of it. One of the major considerations affecting the organization pattern and the degree of development in each step is the listener's present state of understanding and acceptance of the need and the level of belief or controversy that might be present in the speaker's solution. Most persuasion goes beyond making the listener aware of the problem and advocates a course of action to be taken.

Depending on what the speaker is trying to accomplish in his exact purpose, his organization and development may vary.

Consider a number of alternative patterns that may grow out of the speech on "Safe Driving," depending on the exact purpose.

1. *Exact purpose:* To make the listeners aware of the dangers of reckless driving and how this may endanger their lives.

Need or problem development in this speech may comprise almost the entire Body of the speech, in which vivid examples, descriptions, statistics, and other proof will be given to portray the problem. From this, the listener will realize that he must drive carefully and will perhaps not need to be told how to do so. The purpose is largely to arouse feeling and cause action.

2. *Exact purpose:* To have the listener follow specific courses of action in his driving.

Need or problem development here may be brief, but sufficient to make the listener realize how bad the problem is.

Solution or satisfaction development will be considerably longer than in the former speech as the steps in the speaker's plan for safe driving will be explained, supported, and their values emphasized over other methods.

3. *Exact purpose:* To convince the listener that he should vote for a law reducing the speed limit on all highways to fifty miles per hour.

In this speech, the conviction and action asked for will be quite controversial and probably not accepted by the listener initially, requiring that the solution contain more proof, testimony of experts, values, and other development to support the points advocated.

Other methods of organization which chiefly affect the solution part of the persuasive speech may be used after the speaker has first made reference to (or proved) the need or problem. He then may organize his points in the solution by one of the following methods:

This or nothing:

In this method, the speaker tries to prove that all other ways of solving the problem have failed, thus the listener must either follow his solution or nothing. In a speech on a well-recognized problem, it may not be necessary to prove its existence or extent. The chief concern is to find a solution. The main points might be something like this:

Exact purpose: To persuade the listener to favor a specific course of action as the only solution to an accepted problem.

Main points (Body)

I. This problem has been with us a long time and must be solved.
II. Everything we have tried has failed.
  A. . . . has failed.
  B. . . . has failed.
  C. . . . has failed.
III. We must therefore pursue this solution. . . .

Showing positive advantages:

This method is used when the speaker tries to advance a particular solution by proving its advantages over other possible solutions. To a degree, this method is used in many persuasive speeches when the speaker has advanced the problem and offers the audience a number of possible solutions, which he helps them evaluate so that the one he advances is obviously the best. Sometimes he narrows these down to two alternative solutions, Plan A and Plan B. In showing the advantages of Plan B over Plan A, he should organize his points in a systematic sequence, taking up each criterion and discussing each plan under it, such as:

Main points (Body)

I. We are faced with finding a solution to the problem of . . .
II. There have been two major solutions proposed.
   A. Plan A.
   B. Plan B.
III. Which of these should we accept? (indirect method)
   A. Availability of each plan.
      1. Plan A.
      2. Plan B.
   B. Cost of each plan.
      1. Plan A.
      2. Plan B.
   C. Practical operation of each plan.
      1. Plan A.
      2. Plan B.
IV. We thus conclude that Plan B is superior.

Outlining

The completed outline represents the finished structure of the speech. The basic form of a good outline is shown earlier for the "golf ball," which also shows the developed Introduction and Conclusion. We might also point out here that the final outline from which you will plan to practice and present the speech may not achieve complete form until you have considered the developmental tools and methods that are discussed in the next chapter.

Speakers differ as to the degree of detail they want in an outline, both in statement of points and amount of subdevelopment shown under each point. The *topical* form is used for the outline on golf, in which most of the points are stated as brief phrases or words. This is probably sufficient for comparatively simple speech subjects, and when the speaker knows exactly what the phrases mean to him. But in more complex subjects and purposes, it is well to state the main points and some of the subpoints as *full sentences*. They must be crystal clear to you as the speaker or they may never emerge clearly to the listener.

Taking a speech subject such as "Today's Drug Use and Abuse," one main point might be stated in both forms to see the difference in clarity between the sentence and phrase:

I. There is a serious use of drugs among teen-agers today.
   A. Much of this is concentrated in cities.
   B. Drug use in colleges is on the increase.

To handle this outline in phrases may not distinguish the drug topic from any other:

I. Serious problem today. (What problem? For whom?)
   A. Cities. (What about cities and colleges?)
   B. Colleges.

It must be remembered that the outline is a *flexible guide* from which the speech will be given. Its essential value is to help organize your thoughts and materials, after careful analysis of the subject and purpose. It is not to serve as an inflexible pattern from which you cannot deviate. As the speech comes alive, you may need to revise for human interest, timeliness, audience adaptation, or new material discovered. Even the sequence may be changed for some good reason. Another value of the outline is to be able to visualize your speech structure and to insure that every point is where it should be.

SUGGESTIONS FOR OUTLINE FORM

1. *Use large paper on one side only,* so you can spread the sheets out and see all that you are preparing without needing to turn them over.

2. *Have the title, general purpose, and exact purpose in front of you before starting the outline. Include audience analysis.* Keep in mind that all that you put into the outline should help accomplish your purpose.

3. *Organize the main points first and the full Body.* Draft and revise until satisfied.

4. *Show the Introduction, Body, and Conclusion as center headings.*

5. *Use uniform symbols for main and subpoints.* These should be renumbered in each division, particularly so that the Body shows the exact number of main points. Indentations should be clear and consistent, following this form:

Introduction

I. Introductory point.
II. Introductory or transition point.

Body

I. First main point.
   A. Major subpoint.
      1. Subpoint or support.
      2. Subpoint or support.
   B. Major subpoint.
II. Second main point.
III. Third main point.

Conclusion

I. Summary or other concluding point.
II. Concluding point.

6. *Length depends on speaker, subject, and purpose.* There is no rule or formula, as length of outline depends on how much the speaker wants to see on paper.

7. *Leave room at the left of the outline for notes and indicating of methods, steps, and devices used.* Here you can check the sequence used, such as problem-solution-action, whether

you are explaining or proving the point, whether you are using a certain type of support and proof too much or too little, whether you are holding attention and interest (or are likely to).

The Introduction

In your Introduction, strive for the best possible approach in linking your listener to your subject, so that he is interested and receptive to your main ideas and purpose. Starting a speech is like bridging the gap between two people who have just met and who try to get acquainted with each other. These are the methods of a good Introduction:

Get attention of the listener. His mind may be in many other directions, and it must be directed to you and your speech. Your initial manner and enthusiasm are important. Methods of gaining attention in your content are many, including an unusual or startling statement, a thought-provoking question, a reference to a real example or fact, or a brief story if the occasion is suitable. A quotation may be used. In many situations, reference to the occasion, audience, or particular people present may be made.

Use common ground reference to similar experiences, interests and points of view with the audience.

Arouse listener interest in the subject. You cannot assume that his interest is high just because he is present, although good audience analysis prior to the speech should reveal clues to his attitude. The timeliness and importance of the subject *to the listener* should be pointed out. If you have made some reference to his present conditions and experiences, you have no doubt already aroused his interest.

Be brief. The Introduction should take only a few moments at best, and perhaps less.

TRANSITION TO BODY. Listeners want to know when the Body or main points start. Too many speakers simply drift from their opening remarks into a first main point which the listener may awaken to some moments later. There should be a definite overt indication that you are moving from your introductory remarks and into the main part of the speech. To do this clearly, follow these suggestions:

Make an initial summary of the main points at the end of the Introduction and always in the order you will take them up. When you do take up the first point, repeat it and go ahead with its development. However, in a persuasive speech on a controversial subject, it is often best not to indicate your points until you come to each one. You may want to introduce a point more indirectly, such as by raising a question. But even in this situation, many speakers will raise a series of questions as an initial summary to get the listener thinking in the direction of the main points. Persuasion presents many complex considerations of listener attitudes and how to best keep these favorable, or at least not opposed to your points. Yet, as a general principle, listeners like to know what you are talking about.

Continue to consider the value of clear transitions as you move through a speech. Always let your listener know that you are going from one point or division of the speech to another.

The Conclusion

The point we have just made about transitions also concerns the Conclusion. Though you may not want to openly state,

"Now, in conclusion . . ." you should begin closing in a way that seems most comfortable to you. Make it evident that you are ready to draw things together and stop talking. Here are some guidelines:

Summarize what has been said. This is where you "tell them what you've told them" after you first "tell them what you're going to tell them" in the Introduction and transition to the Body. Listeners like to know again what they should take from the speech. This can be done in a clear, point-by-point summary, or in tying together all the points in a paragraph.

Balance points in your favor. In a persuasive speech, the Conclusion should reiterate the values and advantages of your proposals while balancing these with the disadvantages of other courses.

Show future application and action. In an informative speech, the Conclusion should again point the way for the listener to apply the information, such as further reading, applying the points in his future actions, and practicing certain skills. In a persuasive speech, the points made and advocated in the Body may lead to a course of action to be recommended or actually followed.

Do not add new main points. The Conclusion should not start the development of points that have not been taken up in the Body. If it is necessary to develop and support a point, it should be in the Body. Once the audience knows you are started with your Conclusion they expect the speech to end. Thus our next and final suggestion follows.

Be brief. It is wearisome to drag out a Conclusion once you have moved into it. One or two minutes should be sufficient.

VII

DEVELOPING IDEAS

Vague generalities will probably not get you into trouble, nor will they ever accomplish anything; it is the specific and concrete that makes a position clear and meaningful.
—*John Kennedy*

Listeners find it difficult to be interested in ideas that are vague, abstract, and general. Or to understand them. Or to accept them. They want speakers to make ideas concrete and real in order to hold their attention; more specific and clear to have them understood; and with sufficient proof and support to have them accepted. We are presently concerned with the support, development, and proof necessary to make the speech vital and to accomplish its purpose.

Once you have determined your subject and purpose and organized your ideas into a clear sequence of main and subpoints, your next major step in speech preparation is to find the best possible tools and methods to develop them. While quantity of support is important, quality is more so. We are still aiming for short speeches. We don't want listeners to react as Mark Twain did when he sat in church one Sunday morning. At first he so enjoyed the minister's sermon that he decided to put ten dollars in the collection box. But as the speaker rambled on, his mental contribution dwindled to two dollars. Finally, when the collection box reached him hours later, he slyly withdrew two dollars.

Support forms and tools

The most effective speech contains the best available forms or tools of support. *Holding listener interest and attention, achieving clarity and understanding,* and *proving or supporting the point being made* are the major objectives of support materials. The following is a list of the forms of support and the factors or qualities of attention that will make them most effective.

FORMS OR TOOLS OF SUPPORT		FACTORS OR QUALITIES OF ATTENTION AND INTEREST
Facts	Support should	Concreteness
Examples	have as many	Reality
Comparisons or	of these	Familiarity
Illustrations	qualities as	Closeness
Statistics	possible:	Vividness
Testimony or		Striking or unusual
Quotations		Variety
		Vitality
VISUAL AIDS		Humor

It is interesting to note some of the labels applied to the use of support, depending on both speaker's and listener's intent on what the support is to accomplish. We speak of *developing ideas* as the broad label for the total process. We use the term *support* in the sense that the point being made cannot stand alone without providing some means of making it clear or acceptable. Sometimes we question whether there is enough *proof* to prove the point when the point is controversial or tries to move the listener in a particular direction. In this same context, when the speaker is trying to prove a point logically, we refer to his support as *evidence*. Whether or not all or some of these labels are in the listener's mind, the speaker should constantly be aware of the use of support.

Facts. We list facts first as a form of support because listeners think in terms of concrete examples—"Give us some facts" or "Let's get down to cases." Actually it is difficult to define a fact because it can be so many things—statistics, data, reality in the form of specific happenings and instances, and the like. Objective reality is distinguished from judgments, inferences, and opinions peculiar to each speaker. It is the truth. The more specific the use of the forms of support as described in the following paragraphs, the more they are likely to be factual.

"The United States has landed men on the moon."

"New York City has over eight million people. At present it is the largest city in the United States." (The latter statement may be a fact today but not tomorrow.)

It should be noted that facts usually involve concreteness and reality, thus drawing *attention* and *interest*.

Examples. Like a fact, an example is difficult to define because it comes in many different forms. It is basically a reference to an event, situation, place, person, or thing. If every point made by a speaker was supported by one or more examples, the speech would probably be effectively developed. The main considerations in the use of examples are these:

The more specific, concrete, and real they are, the more effective examples will be. Usually the example becomes concrete as the speaker goes from the *general* to the specific reference. In a speech on "Slum Conditions," the following states aspects of the problem in terms of general examples:

"This country's slums extend the length and breadth of the land. We can find them chiefly in large cities. But the small towns are not free of slums, nor are wide sections of the countryside. In the cities, slums frequently exist within a block of attractive business or residential districts."

Development becomes much more meaningful as each general example is reduced to specific concrete places and instances:

"Slum conditions in large cities such as New York, Los Angeles, and Chicago are quite obvious. Yet the extent of these is not always kept in mind. . . . (detail). A walk around New York's Harlem, Los Angeles' Watts district, or Chicago's South Side would reveal some startling facts. . . . In one block in Harlem, one might find . . . (specific vivid detail)."

The detailed specific example adds vividness and concreteness. Usually a speaker will use a greater quantity of examples when the point is in doubt and he wants to prove the acceptance of it. He will probably use fewer but more detailed examples to clarify, arouse emotion, show reality, and project the listener into the situation. Detail is accomplished by description, narrative, and vivid language. Here are some detailed specific examples as *The New York Times* magazine reported them, dealing with "Crime in our Nation's Capitol:"

The 1800 block of Wyoming Avenue, Northwest, provides a remarkable example. It is lined with roomy, turn-of-the-century townhouses and is in the middle of one of Washington's most fashionable neighborhoods. It stands nervously on the edge of the city's black ghetto. In November, muggings had become very frequent. In the last two years, the block has seen two murders, two other serious shootings, and more than 20 holdups. "Right here on the steps of this building," said Tedson J. Meyers, leader of the area citizens committee, "a man was mugged and killed in 1968. Over there a man was mugged and left lying in the dirt. He was pretty bloodied up, lying with his head in the gutter." In front of a red brick house was the spot where at 7 P.M. one evening last March, a 29-year-old educator and Princeton graduate was found dying from a shotgun wound in the chest. The shadows cast by one shrub produced three crimes in one night. After the citizens mounted 60

150-watt floodlights to illuminate the once-shadowy street, these crimes virtually disappeared.

The above paragraph has many elements of concreteness, support, and attention factors. It includes testimony, statistics, and vivid description, all of which is frequently the case when giving the details of an example. Vividness is shown again in this paragraph in the same article:

In parts of Anacostia, block after block of housing projects are boarded up, left to the vandals and rats. In some public housing projects where tenants want to remain but want to get out of the easy reach of prowlers, nobody lives on the ground floor. All the windows are covered with plywood. It is an eerie sight.

The example may be used to develop imagery and mood in the development of a point to stimulate and motivate love of country, as this speech excerpt shows:

What is this love of country we all have so deeply? It is the Mississippi rolling swift and muddy past St. Louis, rolling past Cairo, pouring down past the levees of New Orleans. It is lazy noontide in the pines of North Carolina; it is a sea of wheat rippling in western Kansas. It is the San Francisco peaks far north across the glowing nakedness of Arizona. It is the Grand Canyon and a little stream coming out of a New England ridge. . . .

The hypothetical example is sometimes effective—the speaker assumes a situation or event that does not actually exist and projects the listener into it with as much reality as possible, such as:

"Imagine yourself on the planet Mars (or the moon)."

"If you were walking along a quiet dark street and were suddenly confronted by someone with a gun . . ."

Comparisons or Illustrations. Many comparisons start as examples, often being drawn out as the detail is presented. When a speaker starts with a statement, point, or idea, he may want to clarify it by "illustrating" it with an analogy, story, or anecdote. The illustration is used basically to shed light on the point at hand by comparing it with a situation or example that is clear in the listener's mind. We do this by comparing something difficult with something easy; something unfamiliar with something familiar; something uninteresting with something interesting or familiar.

The simplest form of the illustration is the *analogy* or direct comparison of the point being made with something of a similar nature. One might be explaining or proposing a new plan that is yet unknown or untried. To show that it will work, he compares it with a plan that has worked, such as:

"I believe this plan will work in our company. (Here describe the plan.) It has worked in the Z Company whose plant is similar to ours in size, layout, type of operation, and number of employees. . . . Since this plan is successful there, we can assume it will be here."

When the analogy is factual, it becomes a form of proof, provided the speaker can show that the situation he proposes is much like one already known to the audience. Many speakers use the analogy in more figurative form, chiefly for vividness and for comparing the unknown—the point they are making—with the familiar. Franklin Roosevelt's famous comparison of a three-horse team with the cooperation of the three branches of the federal government is a classic:

"As yet there is no definite assurance that the three-horse team of the American system of government will pull together. If three well-matched horses are put to the task of plowing a field and the team of three pulls as one, the field will be plowed. If one horse lies down in his traces or pulls off in another direction, the field will not be plowed. So it is with the three branches of the government."

Winston Churchill's speeches abound with figurative analogy, frequently in brief form or *simile*. "The German eruption swept like a scythe around our armies." "The blockade of Berlin is an unequal trial of strength. It is like a contest of endurance between two men, one of whom sits quietly grinning in his armchair while the other stands on his head hour after hour." The use of metaphors, as when Churchill said, "This malignancy in our midst must be stamped out," means the use of figurative language—"malignancy"—to quickly develop imagery and actually force the comparison on the listener.

The *story* or *anecdote* is usually used as a comparison in which the speaker applies the point of the story to the point he is making to either clarify or gain acceptance. Stories need not be humorous to accomplish this, although humor may have its place in certain situations and when used appropriately for the audience at hand.

Statistics. Statistics involve the use of figures and data to supply concrete information and to hold interest and attention in developing or proving a point. If your point makes reference to numbers, supply them as accurately, clearly, and vividly as you can. If there is some doubt about their accuracy, cite the source. And by all means, relate them to the audience to make them meaningful. Statistics should be used accurately, but it is sometimes better to give a round figure of "close to $10,000,000" than the exact figure of "$9,989,364.29." It is well to consider using a visual method of showing statistics by either simply putting them on a blackboard or preparing a graph. Repetition of a figure will add to its clarity as well as reinforce its importance. Much the same effect can be gained by contrasting one figure with another. And the interpretation of statistics in terms of audience needs, interests, and feelings will make them much more effective. Here are some examples of their use in speeches:

A speaker discussing the rate of crime increase in Washington (as quoted above in the *Times* examples) used statistics this way. "Meanwhile crime statistics are soaring. In 1966 there were 144 murders; 1968 brought 194; and in 1969 murders increased to 289, a 100% increase in three years. Rapes jumped from 260 in 1968 to 336 in 1969. Robberies were up from 8600 to over 12,000. This orgy of blood and gunsmoke reached a climax on Christmas Eve when, in 24 hours, there were 80 robberies, 42 of them with weapons."

Reducing crimes to rate by minutes, another speaker used these figures. "Data compiled by the FBI reveals this timetable of crimes: A murder every minute; a forcible rape every 23 minutes; a robbery every four minutes; an auto theft every minute; a burglary every 27 seconds. More than 1300 motor vehicles are stolen each day. Since 1960, the total volume of crime has increased 46%, almost six times as fast as the increase in population." (These are 1965 figures.)

William F. Buckley, commenting on college faculty as advisors or administrators in government, said "I'd rather be governed by the first 2000 names in the Boston telephone directory than by the entire Harvard faculty."

Bob Hope used statistics to make a humorous point about the human body and his state of health. "Today my heart beat 103,000 times; my blood traveled 168,000,000 miles; I breathed 23,000 times; I inhaled 438 cubic feet of air; I spoke 4800 words, moved 750 major muscles, and exercised 7,000,-000 brain cells. I'm tired."

A word of caution against a surfeit of statistics, however. When cited too exactly and repeatedly and not related to the audience and the immediacy of the situation, they can be boring and easily ignored by the average listener.

Testimony or Quotation. Testimony backs up the speaker's point by quoting someone in authority in the same field. Quoting such *expert opinion* will reinforce the point in the listener's mind, clarify it, and make him more favorably disposed toward it. Some suggestions and precautions should be observed in using testimony:

▶ The person quoted should be an authority who is recognized by the listeners as such and accepted by them as qualified and reliable.

▶ If in doubt, it is sometimes advisable to indicate the person's background and experience, or the source of the quote, to establish him as an authority.

▶ The statement should be timely and not contradicted at a later date by the person quoted.

▶ The statement should be accurate and not taken out of context.

▶ It should be comparatively brief and preferably read rather than memorized or paraphrased in the speaker's own words.

Some of these suggestions may not be applicable when a quotation is used to make your point more vivid or emphatic. Sometimes you can find a statement by an outstanding person recognized by the audience in which the authority used unusual and picturesque language to express a thought you are trying to express. Ministers frequently quote from the Bible, and lay speakers can do this as well. John F. Kennedy's famous "Ask not what your country can do for you; ask what you can do for your country" and Patrick Henry's "Give me liberty or give me death" could be used for great effect or emphasis to reinforce a speaker's point.

The cumulative use of testimony can be very effective when it is deemed helpful to quote a series of authorities, especially when a speaker's point may not be accepted by his audience. He might say, "My proposal is not merely a hasty or unconsidered idea on my part. It has been weighed carefully and endorsed by leading figures and authorities, including those from business and industry, government, and labor. Henry Ford II recently made this statement . . . The Secretary of the Treasury said . . .

George Meany, president of the AFL-CIO has stated his position similarly . . ."

Quantity or quality? The very matter of speech length will limit the number of support tools, thus demanding that the speaker search for those with highest quality. But he should have a storehouse of material from which he can select the best. The speech is somewhat like the visible part of an iceberg with that beneath forming the foundation and reservoir of material for that which shows.

Aristotle developed his three proofs of a speaker's effectiveness and influence: ethical, logical, and emotional.

Ethical proof (*ethos*) is composed of the total personal qualities of the speaker that help influence his listener to accept his ideas, points, and purpose. Recent studies on use of evidence and proof show that if an audience likes and respects a speaker as a person, he will have to use less evidence and proof to have them accept his point. Another way of saying this is that if you like and respect a speaker, you will tend to like what he says.

Logical proof is the speaker's use of sound reasoning and evidence in attempting to influence the thought process of the listener.

Emotional proof is the speaker's attempt to influence the feelings and emotions of the listener by appealing to his basic wants and drives. Both logical and emotional proof or appeal are fundamental to accomplishing persuasion and motivation and are discussed in Chapter VIII.

Visual aids

The primary use of visual aids is to clarify and support the point being made orally by the speaker, as well as to better hold attention and interest. It is sometimes difficult to make an idea clear by words alone, and indeed, considering the impact of today's visual media, a picture is worth far more than a thousand words. One should not think of visual aids as a substitute for oral discourse, however. It is almost always essential to accompany their use with verbal explanation and comment.

The most common aids used while speaking are the blackboard or chart easel on which the speaker may develop material as he is speaking; that is, write out key points, draw a diagram, make a chart, or show figures and statistics. He may also use objects, models, demonstrations, or charts prepared in advance of the speech. Pictures and handouts are important forms, as well as slides or videotape or film.

These suggestions should be followed in using visual aids:

1. Consider, in making any point in a speech, whether some form of visual aid may help make it clear, reinforce it, or make it more interesting.

2. Plan in advance the use of any aid, and when and how you will integrate its use with the spoken word.

3. In using the blackboard or chart easel for developmental purposes, be sure it is clean and in a good position relative to the audience. Plan what your material will look like as it develops and when it is finished by putting it on paper in your speech preparation. Print or write uniformly in large bold letters. Don't hide your work with your body. Turn frequently toward your listeners and look at them while developing your material. Raise the voice projection level if you have to occasionally talk into the board. Keep talking while working at the board, and don't allow long periods of silence. Stand away and use a pointer or the arm extended while explaining what is on the board.

4. A chart easel pad may be used in lieu of the blackboard with the advantage that each chart may be torn off and hung separately if desired, and they may be kept for a summary after the speech.

5. Do not leave blackboard, chart material, or any other form of visual aid in back of you as you speak, unless this

material is directly related to the point being made at the time. If the material is not related, it will pull the attention of your listeners toward the material and away from what you will be saying.

6. In using charts prepared in advance, time their use to bring them out in conjunction with the point being reinforced.

7. In using models or objects, hold them up in clear view of the audience or place them on a table for all to see. Walk toward or into the audience with them as appropriate, for closer viewing.

8. In using handout materials, time their distribution with the point being made and keep attention in focus on the point. Caution the audience not to read while you are speaking. If the material is complex and you want the audience to be familiar with it in advance, plan to distribute the handouts well before you speak.

9. In using slides, videotape, or motion pictures, view them in advance and plan your discussion and comments on each in advance. Maintain directness and good voice projection with your audience. Prepare key questions for discussion immediately after viewing a videotape or film.

Attention and interest factors

We again emphasize the importance of using support that has maximum qualities of attention and interest for your particular audience. Valuable support is *concrete, specific,* with the added quality of being *familiar* and/or *close.* An example might be realistic yet might not be as effective as one that happened nearby or is well known and can strike a familiar reaction. And if the example, comparison, or quotation is *unusual* or couched in terms and language that is *striking* or *humorous,* or has a *vital* appeal to basic emotions, this will gain attention over a support tool that does not have these qualities.

In considering the use of examples, statistics, testimony, and other support tools, there are at least two major principles that affect both attention and proof. The first is that of *variety*, which is a fundamental factor of attention in that we lose interest when we hear too much of the same thing. The other seemingly opposing principle is that of *cumulation*, which suggests that a series of examples or testimonials, one after another, will have a good cumulative effect in proving a point and gaining acceptance of it. The speaker must determine which principle will prevail in the given point development.

Vividness pertains chiefly to language. The good speaker makes an attempt to use *imagery* in his speech development and wording so that he will stimulate as many of the listener's senses as possible, and the listener in turn *sees, hears, tastes, smells,* and *touches* what is being said. This helps develop a stronger feeling of *empathy* with the speaker and his points.

Summary of support methods and forms

In presenting this summary, we are attempting to show the methods of development and support most used when the purpose is to inform as compared with the purpose to persuade. We must keep in mind, however, that these overlap to a great extent and that both purposes may exist within the same speech, particularly in the development of a specific point.

IN INFORMATIVE SPEAKING (to achieve clarity and understanding)	IN PERSUASIVE SPEAKING (to influence beliefs, feelings, and actions)
These methods most used: Explanation Definition Description Narration Demonstration	*These methods most used:* Informative methods (mostly explanation, definition, and sometimes others) Reasoning Appeal to emotions

Supported by:
Examples
Comparisons
Statistics
Visual Aids

Supported by:
(For reasoning and logical
proof)
Examples in greater number
Testimony as expert opinion
Facts and statistics
Analogy
Visual aids
(For appeal to emotions and
motivation)
Examples in more vivid detail
Illustrations with human
interest
Quotation with vivid language
Imagery and appeal to senses
Visual aids

Both repetition and cumulation should be considered in using development methods and support. *Repetition* is sometimes regarded as a form of support in that it reinforces the point being made, either for increased clarity and understanding or for greater emphasis and acceptance. It is often effective to repeat a statement, a figure in using statistics, or a testimonial. Repetition may be in the exact form of the original or in similar language, perhaps preceded by, "In other words . . ." "To say this again in different language . . ." or simply, "To repeat . . ." It is also well to repeat in making internal summaries during a speech and a final summary at the end. *Cumulation* has been explained above as the use of the same form of support in series, such as a long series of specific examples or testimonials in developing a point. The repeated use of the same form of support has an excellent effect toward gaining acceptance of the point.

Direct or indirect method. In most situations, particularly in informing and making a point clear, the speaker first states the point, and possibly its subpoints, then offers his support and proof of it. When there is controversy and the listener is not apt to agree or accept the point initially, the speaker can lead toward it more indirectly or inductively by using a question or series of questions, or by making a transition. The next chapter on persuasion further discusses this method.

VIII

MOTIVATING, PERSUADING, AND SELLING

More men have talked their way up the ladder of success than have climbed it in any other way.

—*Bruce Barton*

Motivating and influencing listeners may well be the goal of all communication, speeches in particular. Motivation and persuasion are difficult to distinguish, for each may include the other, and they may both mean the same thing.

Motivation is the movement of the listener's interests, attitudes, feelings, and beliefs toward some kind of response in the direction of the speaker's subject and purpose. Every good speech should motivate the listener in some way, at the least to arouse his interest and to provoke favorable attitudes. To the extent his beliefs are influenced, his desires stimulated, his understanding made more clear, or he is moved to action, what he hears has motivated him in some way.

Persuasion similarly deals with influence; within this broad definition a listener may be influenced to understand, as in a speech to inform. But understanding alone is not enough. Most of the time when we think of persuasion as a speech objective, we have a definite predetermined purpose to *influence* attitudes, beliefs, feelings, and actions; unless, of course, the understanding itself moves the listener to believe, feel, or act in the direction of the speaker's purpose. Persuasion may have as its goal influencing the listener to accept and approve a proposal, plan, or new piece of legislation, to gain acceptance of a new policy, to sell a product, or even to get his wife to stay home instead of going to the movies.

Selling is the primary concern of the sales or marketing person who must move his product for a living. But we are always selling in our daily lives as communicators, and primarily we and our beliefs are the product.

Motivation

There are many reasons why listeners are not motivated during a speech. They may lack interest in the subject, may be quite apathetic toward it because of ignorance or misunderstanding, or they may fail to see any connection between themselves and what the speaker is saying. The listener could hold actual negative attitudes, either about the speaker, his purpose, or the points he is trying to make. Possibly these are due to a stated conviction about a subject or, more likely, to an unstated resistance we develop to any change in the *status quo* since most of us want to do things as we have been doing them. Fear of the possible results of the proposals of a speaker who is upsetting tradition may hold the listener back, especially if the speaker fails to show the rewards and benefits that will come from his persuasion.

Motivation is the attempt, then, to move the listener in positive directions in all these respects. In doing this, the speaker will:

Gain and hold attention and interest by using as many of the principles and tools of support in his development as possible, constantly applying these to the listener.

Get on common ground by using material that shows how the speaker's points share the listener's interests, experiences, needs, and wants.

Relate points and material to basic wants and drives that will appeal to the listener.

Keep his entire speech content and development related to the *you* position of the listener, not the *I* or *self* position of the speaker.

Vital appeals and drives

Human motivation is tied very much to the basic drives, wants, and motives that all of us have and that influence our decisions and actions. While most of us like to claim that we do everything for some logical reason and that our thinking process is sound, it is more likely to be wants that affect our actions. Good speakers will therefore try to tie the points they are making to the drives and needs of their audience.

While attempting this, realize also that each of us possesses a different "mix" of these drives. All of us have the strong need to exist, to live, to have physical safety and well-being and in a situation where this is threatened, such as an accident or fire, we would all act to save our lives. But some would feel the loss of a library more strongly than the loss of a color television set.

Basic human wants and drives are operative at a given time because of many influencing factors, including the concern for *self;* the influence of the *environment*, which includes relations with associates and friends both social and business, rivalry and competition, and comfort and pleasure; and the *goals* to which one aspires, whether high or low, economic or social, status-related or not. The astute speaker will attempt to analyze and assess the way and degree that these are active in the speech situation.

There are many lists and classifications of the basic human wants, drives, or emotions. The following list is representative, though we make no attempt to show them in order of importance.

Life or self-preservation: The desire to live is fundamental. It includes not only the need to survive but to have a level of existence commensurate with one's concept of self. We thus include the need for air, shelter, and food as parts of this drive. The efforts of many to improve the air we breathe and to rid ourselves of air and water pollution are tied to this drive. In a speech to inform by instruction, an instructor in an Air Force parachute training school achieved maximum motivation of his listeners when he met a group at 6 A.M. one morning. He came into the room and threw a pack on the table and said, "Gentlemen, this is a newly invented parachute. It has never been tried or used before by a human being. At seven A.M. each of you will put one of these on his back and drop out of a plane at ten thousand feet. I am now going to instruct you on how to use this parachute." There was no question of attention and interest. This message had built-in motivation to survive. Either they listened and understood, or their lives were in danger.

Property and material possessions: All of us have this basic drive, yet the degree may vary from the beggar who is content with enough money to survive to the ambitious young man who "wants to make a million." On the other side, this drive also includes that of economy, practicality, and workability. Much modern advertising is directed specifically in these directions, and the speaker should be well aware of their significance in planning his proof and support.

Power or ego-expansion: Most of us want to achieve a degree of power that will satisfy our own ego and give us a feeling of security and even of authority. This need is very much related to the drive for property, and is the drive that motivates a person to achieve higher status in his work, profession, or social relations. It moves some to seek political office or an executive position in their company. The college faculty member who is now an instructor or associate professor strives to publish or become well known so that he may one day become a full professor. In informing and explaining, speakers can make listeners aware that the information they impart will give them knowledge that may lead to greater power and status; or in proposing a course of action, the speech can be made attractive in terms of the rewards to the listener.

Reputation and self-esteem: We all want to be respected and admired by our fellow man, regardless of the environment in which we spend most of our business or social time. Usually we will go out of our way to accept a proposal or do something that is shown by a speaker to have a likely influence on what others think of us. We may thus be motivated to join a certain organization, support a cause, run for an office, make a speech, or buy certain clothes, any or all of which may improve the regard that other people have for us.

Affections and sentiments: We come to more intangible motives that are very much a part of ourselves. These motives include the most fundamental emotion of love of family and dear ones, friendship and respect we feel for others, and our concern for the human race as a whole. And along with these feelings there are the many emotions we experience in most of our waking hours—happiness, sadness, pleasure, sympathy, fear, gladness, sorrow, love, hate. Sex is of course a major human want and might be placed at the top of any list. It is today a seemingly more open matter both in discussion and in action, and many would-be persuaders try to link sex drives with almost every purpose to be accomplished, especially in advertising and marketing where it is emphasized to bring out a need for a particular product.

Aesthetic tastes: The influence of beauty and fineness is very strong in most of us. We enjoy good music, literature, paintings, architecture. We spend money for all these; we may even stand in line in the rain or cold to buy a ticket for a particular event.

There are many opportunities for speakers to link their points with such tastes, and they are tied closely to our affections and sentiment.

Appeals to the senses through vivid imagery and description, the use of human interest examples and stories in detail to stimulate the emotions can all lead to greater listener motivation. It perhaps should be pointed out that when a speaker is appealing to an emotional want or drive, he usually does not tell his audience that he is doing this. His development is such that the motivation is touched off through the listener's natural response, not a manufactured one.

Persuasion

We have already defined persuasion as influence, and we continue our discussion of this most important speech objective which in many ways encompasses all the rest. We have discussed persuasion in regard to speech purposes in Chapter V, to organization patterns and outlining in Chapter VI, and to development and support in Chapter VII. In some of this previous discussion, we have indicated that influence may be accomplished through the speaker's person, image, or *ethos*, through use of *logical* reasoning and proof, and through appeal to *emotional* and basic drives.

But a speaker does not decide whether his dominant development and proof is to be logical- or emotional-motivated simply by his own whim. Most speeches can be a happy combination of both, as a result of thorough analysis of audience and goals and use of the best available materials and resources at hand. Yet the degree to which influence is accomplished through logic or emotion may well depend on the *relation of the listener's attitude to the speaker's exact purpose*. We refer to this relation as the "ladder of belief" prior to the speech, and hence the extent to which the speaker must win over belief during the speech. If acceptance of the speaker's purpose is high but apt to be dormant, the speaker may try to *stimulate* the listener to believe more strongly. If the level of belief is low, the speaker may have to *convince* the listener. Another way to explain this is to "divide" the process of persuasion as follows:

We must CONVINCE when the level of acceptance in the listener is low, such as in controversial purposes and points, making use mostly of *logical proof* through sound reasoning, support, and proof.	We must STIMULATE and MOTIVATE when the level of belief may be high but is dormant or apathetic, making most use of *emotional proof* through appeal to basic wants and drives.	We may accomplish ACTION response through either or both.

Examples of speech purposes to *convince,* indicating controversy or possible low levels of acceptance or belief:

Invest in the stock market.

Buy a foreign car.

The "domino theory" in Asia is sound.

Men are more logical than women.

Vacation to Europe rather than in the United States.

Mass protest by students is warranted.

Examples of speech purposes more to *stimulate* and *motivate,* where the level of acceptance is high but dormant or apathetic:

Patriotism and love of country are important.

Drive carefully.

Good health depends on diet and exercise.

Everyone needs some religion.

Students have the right to free speech.

It might be interesting to change or write any of the above in more detail so that a purpose that seems controversial might become one that is accepted, particularly by certain audiences. In doing so, state the purpose and the audience and to what degree you think it requires conviction, stimulation, and motivation.

Most persuasive speeches follow an *organization pattern* or sequence of specific steps, with varying degrees of development on each depending on the purpose, degrees of belief at each stage, and other factors.

SEQUENCE IN PERSUASION

1. Draw attention toward the subject.
2. Indicate the problem, need, or situation.
3. Analyze the problem's origin, history, causes, manifestations.
4. Lead toward possible solutions, or mention them.
5. Lead toward most desired solution or action.
6. Offer proof and values of solution proposed.
7. Prove it as better than other solutions, will eliminate causes of problems, will work, and has values.
8. Lead toward desired response from audience.
9. Show how desired response can be realized.
10. Conclude by summary and "appeal" as appropriate.

Straight or logical thinking

Logical proof, usually used to convince, consists of sound reasoning and good use of evidence or support. Straight thinking starts with a systematic approach to speech preparation that involves the steps of planning, organizing, and developing for best clarity and effect. When a speaker determines exactly what he wants to accomplish with a particular audience and the order in which he will do it, he has taken a major step toward straight and logical thinking.

The three major requirements of logical thinking are: (a) to know the difference between fact and inference; (b) to know the forms or processes of reasoning and whether they are being used soundly; (c) to use good and sufficient evidence or proof.

1. *The fact-inference distinction* is vital. A fact is usually true and accepted by the listener as true. When a speaker is simply stating facts to inform listeners he should anticipate no lack of belief or controversy (unless he has low *ethos* with the group or there are reasons to doubt that he is telling the truth). But when he uses facts from which to draw judgments, opinions, or inferences, he should realize that his listeners may not necessarily draw the same conclusions from them. *Reasoning, then, is the process of drawing inferences (judgments, opinions, conclusions, beliefs are all words having similar meaning) from facts or from other inferences.* If the facts are true or if the other inference is established and accepted by the audience, the reasoning is apt to be sound. But it is most important that the speaker know when he is using the reasoning process, and he must try to anticipate whether his listeners agree or disagree with his line of reasoning.

2. *The processes of reasoning* are somewhat related and intertwined, frequently making it difficult to ascertain whether the speaker is reasoning *inductively* or *deductively*.

Inductive reasoning is the process of drawing inferences from facts. Another way to say this is to describe induction as reasoning from the specific to the general. If restaurant chain A serves you a good meal once and you come away happy with another chain A restaurant, you may generalize that "All meals in restaurant chain A are good." Whether such an inference is sound might depend on at least two tests: Have you experienced *enough* examples, and have they been *representative* of the total? Actually, what a speaker usually does with the inductive process is to state the generalization (opinion, belief) as a main point and then use the examples as support. This is one of the most common forms of reasoning.

Analogical reasoning, which we have discussed concerning comparisons and analogies in Chapter VII, is another form of the inductive process. We draw a conclusion about the item we are discussing by comparing it to something similar. The inference is sound if the two are sufficiently alike.

Causal reasoning, or drawing a conclusion that an existing fact (cause) will produce a yet unknown result (effect), is a form used in most of our daily thinking. We say that this fertilizer (fact) will cause thick green grass (effect); that X candidate will cause good conditions for our city if elected; or that this medicine will cause us to get well. We also reason from a known effect and try to conclude what caused it. We may have a stomach-ache and reason that it was caused by certain food we ate; or we note that the ground is wet in the morning and reason that it rained during the night. In more complex situations, such as social unrest in today's world, it is much more difficult to ascertain the cause. The following questions contest the soundness of causal reasoning. Could the cause have produced the claimed effect by itself? Did some other cause intervene? Are other aspects of the cause-effect relationship logical?

Deductive reasoning is the process of drawing inferences or conclusions from the general to the specific. In other words, once a generalization has been established, we try to fit a particular specific into it. Having concluded that all restaurant chain A meals are good, we drive into one in a new city and predict that "this will be a good meal" and hope that our deduction will be sound. Or we have concluded the generalization, after examining many facts and specifics, that computers add to the efficiency of large business organizations. We can thus approach business Z and reason that "computers will be good for your business too." Obviously, all such deductions are based on a sound general premise first arrived at by the inductive process. For the deduction to be sound, the premise or generalization on which it is based must be sound; the specific instance must fit totally and accurately into the generalization; and the conclusion drawn (the deduction) must be the same as (and thus limited to) that of the major premise.

The reasoning process is complex and much more so than we indicate in this brief explanation. The student of logic will go further to understand it and to know whether his own thinking is clear. Yet the practical tests that must be met both in his mind and the listener's are whether his statements are facts and information or whether they are inferences and opinions; if inferences, whether those drawn by the speaker are sufficiently proved and supported by evidence and made with sufficient soundness in relation to other inferences or facts to be accepted.

We keep reminding the would-be persuader that he has in his person perhaps the most powerful tool for influencing others and that his *personal proof value* (*ethos*) may be strong enough to compensate for lack of evidence or occasional inferences and conclusions that would otherwise not be accepted. The principle "If I like you as a person I will tend to like what you say" works in favor of the speaker who presents himself in the most favorable light to a particular audience.

Special methods in persuasion

We have already referred to most of the methods, but we will now summarize them and add a few more.

Common ground is the attempt on the part of the speaker to connect his subject, purpose, points, support, and language to the listener's interests, experiences, and beliefs. A common tie is exceedingly important in the Introduction of a speech to arouse the listener's interest and have him feel that the speaker is concerned with him—use the *you*-centered approach in starting a speech and continue it throughout. Utilize the factors of attention that are familiar, close, and vital to the listener and point out ideas and opinions in which both you, as speaker, and the listener share.

Indirectness is coupled with *suggestion* as a primary method of gaining favorable listener response if the point may not be accepted by direct proof. *The best persuasion occurs when the listener himself arrives at the belief or feeling that the speaker wants him to have.* It is then *his* idea . . . not just the speaker's. And when such a conclusion is reached by a listener *himself* he will feel or believe it much more strongly. In using this method, the speaker will make a transition to his purpose or point by perhaps raising a *question,* citing examples or other facts, or offering a comparison. He will use as much support and evidence as he thinks necessary for the listener to draw his own inferences. A good rule of thumb is to use this indirect method when the point is controversial. For clarity the speaker will usually state his point and then offer his development and support. But if he uses the indirect method of suggestion, he should be sure that the listener gets the point before he leaves it. Too often speakers leave the listener uncertain or confused as to just what the point was.

Exaggeration or overstatement may sometimes be effective for gaining attention and interest, or even motivating the listener. But use it cautiously and not in such way that the listener will think the speaker to be unreliable or unethical.

Polarizing an audience occurs when an attempt is made to arouse uniform strong emotional response among everyone present. In certain situations and occasions where emotions run deep on a particular subject, a total group response might be achieved. Emotional appeal is frequently sought at the expense of logic and reason. One associates polarizing with propaganda and mass psychology methods used by those who would try to shut out logical thought in favor of the fervor and excitement that aroused emotions can bring. Hitler was perhaps the greatest master of this kind of persuasion. Included among his methods was the complete surrounding of the audience by visuals to create a desired mood, masses of people in great halls, the booming sounds of both music and the speaker's voice, repetition of slogans, exaggerated statements—and the physical and emotional excitement of the speaker. While hardly techniques to be used by the average speaker, rational polarization may be achieved by continued use of cumulation as a support method, the repeated use of the same form of support or appeal to wants and desires, and vivid language.

Quiet and subdued conciliation may be more effective in small groups where logical thought can prevail. Here a soft conciliatory manner, some making of concessions, narrowing of points of differences, use of common ground, indirect method or direct method used without dogmatism, and a pleasant use of voice all may combine to achieve the maximum persuasion.

Yes-response is the technique of arranging the sequence of points, their introduction into the speech, and method of development in such way that the listener will always be responding "yes." He will continue this response all the way to the speaker's ultimate proposal or purpose.

Selling as persuasion

Selling is persuasion. Everything we have said up to now about persuasion would also apply for getting people to buy something. There is very little difference between the objective of a salesman trying to sell a product, a wife selling her husband on the idea of going to a party together, or a candidate selling himself in pleading for approval of his platform and for votes.

The typical pattern of the sales presentation or interview follows the same sequence as the ten steps in persuasion we presented above. Sometimes they take on slightly different labels to emphasize the sales situation and goal:

1. Approach to prospect related to physical setting.
2. Attention and interest aroused; common ground.
3. Arouse need and desire (problem).
4. Show product as satisfying need (solution).
5. Show advantages and values.
6. Meet and overcome objections.
7. Lead toward close or sale of product.

In the two columns below, we show the attempt of two salesmen to sell an oil burner, the one being quite negative, the other using positive persuasion. Which one got the sale?

Salesman 1

"This oil burner will be a very efficient heating system. It has many advantages over your old system. If you buy it, we can install it without too much trouble. We'll have to tear out your coal bin and get the coal out of your basement through the kitchen. Chances are we'll have to break a large hole in your basement wall in order to install the oil tank, since it won't go through

Salesman 2

"When you consider the dirt and dust from your present coal furnace, both in the basement and throughout the house, it's almost unbelievable to compare this with the cleanliness of oil heat. There isn't a speck of dust from oil, and the fuel is delivered inside your house from a truck at the curb. The small oil tank takes up only a fraction of the space of your coal bin and attracts no dirt at the door. That shouldn't be too much trouble, however. One of the other problems is tearing up your front lawn and making a ditch through which we can run the oil pipeline. Now, with regard to the thermostat, this will require making a hole in the plaster in the living room wall. This can be patched up again without much trouble. The whole thing shouldn't take more than a couple of days of inconvenience on your part. It will cost you six hundred dollars."

all. You can hang clothes in the basement with no concern for coal dust or ashes. The oil burner operates almost silently. You never have to shake grates, and you'll never have a stuck clinker. The thermostat control is placed in a convenient location and the flip of a thumb gives you quick, silent, efficient heat. It takes only a short time to install our equipment. This can be done during a day while you are out on a shopping trip. We can arrange monthly payments which you will hardly notice."

4

You as a Communicator

IX. DELIVERY: COMMUNICATING A SPEECH

X. LISTENING

IX

DELIVERY: COMMUNICATING A SPEECH

> All attempts of moving the feelings must prove ineffectual
> unless they be enlivened by the voice of the speaker, by his
> look, and by the action of his whole body.
>
> —*Quintilian*

You now have most of your speech under your belt. You've
planned and built it step by step, gaining confidence as you
prepared. And you hold a finished outline in your hand with
much of its contents in your head as a part of your thought
process. Now you are ready for delivery of the speech—to
communicate the message you have prepared to the audience
for whom it was intended.

Think back to Chapter II and your answer to its question,
"What kind of speaker do you want to be?" Also recall our
analysis of the communicator in today's society, the nature of
the audience of the 1970s—informed and participative—not to
be "talked down to" but eager to "talk things over" with a
speaker. And recall some of the things you *do not want to be*
when you speak:

► Not an orator.

► Not a performer or actor.

► Not merely giving an exercise in voice and expression.

► Not merely saying words from memory or a manuscript.

► Not expecting to be too calm so as to be indifferent or
unenthusiastic.

▶ Not avoiding or expecting not to have a degree of healthy nervous energy.

▶ Not trying to pattern after any "ideal" or "model" speaker.

Practicing the speech

Though the amount is closely related to individual needs and habits, there are three major reasons for practicing a speech:

1. *To absorb the speech* and become thoroughly familiar with the main points, subpoints, and support material so that they are part of you and quickly come to mind (or from notes) as the speech progresses.

2. *To develop language facility* by verbalizing aloud, hearing yourself, and using flexible choice of words.

3. *To refine and improve* your delivery, not just for mechanics or performance but for total effectiveness in manner, projection, variety, and emphasis. In fact, a new, separate science called *kinesics* has developed in this area to encompass the study of body language, i.e., the use of our physical selves—expression, manner, gesture—in communication.

When to practice. The sooner the better. Just like speech preparation, practice should be spread out over a number of days. You'll be more confident if you spend half an hour a day for six days than three hours the night before you are to speak. There is a period of maturation during which the speech gradually becomes a part of your thought process, and you will find yourself thinking about it—even verbalizing ideas—as you walk down the street or sit at home. You will develop more familiarity and facility as you make changes and become more comfortable with the speech itself.

How to practice. In the first stage of practice you are primarily concerned with making the speech part of your thought process. For some, this involves fixing and absorbing the ideas in the memory for recall; others will rely more on notes during the speech and will do very little if any memorizing. This is the sequence of steps in the first stages of practice:

1. Go completely through the outline several times to get a total impression of the speech as it unfolds.

2. Take each main point in the Body of the speech and go through it, first silently but then aloud. You will determine whether you plan to state the point directly and then develop it or use an indirect method in the actual speech presentation. Determine how long each point will take. Think of transitions from one point to another.

3. Now go through the entire Body again with the time factor in mind.

4. Speak through the Conclusion and try to conclude several ways.

5. Speak through the Introduction, leaving some flexibility for adapting to the chairman and occasion.

6. As you are practicing, you will work toward the development of a set of notes, as we point out later in this chapter.

Consider the following cautions and suggestions regarding how you practice:

Not only silently: If one has thorough knowledge of his subject and strong verbal facility, he may do a good job of the speech without ever practicing it aloud. But if he finds himself speaking the ideas aloud for the first time when he is in front of his audience, he may not have the fluency of language he thought he had. It is therefore well for most of us to find a place where we can comfortably speak through the speech aloud.

Not only seated: Initially, one might go through the speech while seated at a desk. But if the speaker hasn't actually practiced on his feet, he may suddenly find his composure evaporating when he faces his audience. Thinking on your feet, the essence of good speaking, becomes thinking *aloud* on your feet—and that requires practice. Ultimately, the novice speaker may find his thought processes actually improving as he stands. At the same time, of course, he develops two other vital facets: delivery and projection.

Not in front of a mirror: If you look at yourself when you practice, you become more concerned with your appearance, posture, and gesture than you should. The mirror forces self-centeredness and can imply one-way communication. Thus, if you are to use it at all, do not do so in the early stages of practice and not to any great extent.

To a friend?: We put a question mark here, for there may be some value in practicing the speech on a friend to get his opinion and ascertain whether you are really communicating. But it is not recommended in the early stages of speech practice when you are trying to absorb the points and gain fluency. The presence of one person as a listener can be a distraction at this point. But one should try to talk over the speech in conversation with a friend, for it helps the speaker gain flexibility and fluency in verbalizing his ideas. And in the later stages of practice, it might be valuable (and comfortable) for some speakers to present the entire speech to a small group of friends or associates. Many organizations insist that this be done as a sort of "dry run" in which the colleagues pass judgment, make suggestions for improvement, and even give the speaker added confidence.

In the actual room: Though it may be very difficult to practice your speech in the room where it will be given, you should try to simulate the setting if at all possible. It can add greatly to your confidence. In any case, plan to go to the speech setting early. Give yourself sufficient time to look over the room, the equipment, the speaker's stand or podium, the size of the listening group. You will be able to determine the degree of projection needed, placement of visual aids and notes, and need for a microphone.

Amount of practice: No one can tell you how much to practice a speech. Some instructors recommend that the average speaker go through his speech aloud ten times, but there is no set rule. How familiar are you with this subject? Have you spoken on it before? Can you readily verbalize your main and subpoints and their support? What is your normal facility for verbalizing ideas in your everyday contacts? How confident are you that you are ready to communicate this speech to others? How strongly do you believe in your ideas and purpose? These and other questions will affect the amount of practice you need.

Too much practice can lead to staleness and can take away some of the natural conversational manner and enthusiasm. It can also lead to memorization, which is exactly what oral discourse is not. You should not try to remember the exact way you voiced a thought each time you practice it, except for unusual statements that you feel you have perfected. Occasionally, such a wording might be written verbatim into your notes, but your practice should promote flexible choice of language.

Practicing to refine and improve delivery: The average person will not need to work for refinement of delivery once the speech has become part of his thought process and he feels the desire to communicate the message. He will naturally show the animation and enthusiasm that brings appropriate projection, force, emphasis, and gesture.

A tape or cassette recorder is very helpful in timing the speech, analyzing content, and working toward voice improvement. Obvious matters such as monotone, lack of emphasis, sluggish or hurried pacing, poor use of pauses, sloppy articulation, and poor pronunciation can be picked up and corrected.

Presenting the speech

You've come a long way in readying yourself to communicate your speech to others. Your *attitude* is a key factor in your desire to communicate, as we discussed in an earlier chapter.

► Use nervous energy to advantage and in a positive manner. Accept the fact that everyone has it and that the major factor is its CONTROL. Direct it toward the kind of enthusiasm and energy so vital to good speech communication. Your preparation and practice are major keys in turning nervous energy to positive use and gaining confidence in your ability to use it.

Physical control of nervous energy is sometimes assisted by taking a deep breath or two before you are introduced to speak, by approaching the speaker's stand in a firm manner, pausing and looking at your audience, beginning with a degree of projection and animation that will let yourself go, using gesture, changing position occasionally (but not randomly), and bringing appropriate notes with you to give an added measure of confidence.

These suggestions have to do with your *physical manner:*

► In approaching the speaker's stand, show that you are alive and have sufficient energy to make this speech. Stand solidly and comfortably on both feet, not leaning on one or the other or with a knee bent. Normally you would not lean on the speaker's stand unless the situation is very informal. Put your hands on the stand if you like. But do not keep them there throughout the speech and do not hold onto the lectern for dear life. If it is more comfortable, keep your hands at your sides, but not as if you're a soldier about to salute. And keep your hands out of your pockets, since this gives an impression of indifference that can only be overcome by extreme enthusiasm and projection. The hands should never be tied down in any one position that will inhibit or prevent the use of natural gesture. An occasional hand in a pocket may be all right!

▶ Pause and look at specific people in your audience before saying a word. Gain their eye contact and attention initially and keep it.

▶ Place your notes on the stand—or, better if feasible, put them there before the meeting starts.

▶ Begin talking to your audience, after proper response to the chairman, as though conversing with certain individuals from time to time.

▶ Use a level of voice projection that you know can easily be heard by those in the last row. But keep some in reserve for emphasis, meaning, and variety.

▶ Let your nervous energy infuse your animation and enthusiasm so that gestures and facial and bodily expression will come as naturally as in an informal face-to-face discussion with a friend.

▶ Don't think about when and how you use gesture. They will be a part of your natural total communicative manner when you want to emphasize or otherwise help communicate meaning through their use.

▶ Don't wander about aimlessly, but change your position from time to time in order to be more comfortable, get closer to your listeners, or to make a major transition in the thought content of the speech.

▶ Pause as needed to let a point sink in. This pause gives the listener time to think and indicates oral punctuation, which is as necessary in speaking as commas, periods, exclamation marks, and question marks are in writing.

► Make clear transitions from point to point by pauses, internal summaries, and such words as "first," "second," "in addition, let's consider."

► Glance at your notes without interrupting direct communication with the audience.

Suggestions for using notes

Most speakers use notes of some sort. We have already implied that notes in themselves do not make for bad speaking or poor communication, but they can interfere if they are overused or are in a form that calls undue attention to them. We make these suggestions:

► Put notes on small cards, about four by six inches. Do not use large paper or bring along the whole speech outline. Avoid the use of thin paper that makes a distracting noise. You do not want to try to hide the fact that you are using notes, but you do not want to flaunt them either.

► Use only one side of the card or paper and put it aside or under the others when you are finished with it. Turning over notes calls too much attention to them. And if you insist on using your large paper outline, do not fasten it together so that you must—obviously and noisily—flip over each sheet as you finish with it. This is among the sloppiest ways of using notes.

► Put key words or ideas, not full sentences or great detail, on the notes to represent your points. Remember that you are to become familiar with your points in practice and not to rely on notes constantly. Three or four cards should be enough.

► Put figures, statistics, testimony, quotations or other specific facts on the notes. Do not try to memorize them. It is often more effective to read this type of material from the cards to give it more authenticity.

▶ Do not try to conceal notes from your audience by folding them in the palm of your hand or in your pocket. They will know you have them and are using them anyway. But refer to them only when you need to and keep your eyes and your hands off them. Remember that your communication is with your listeners and they should command your eye contact 99 per cent of the time.

▶ Become so familiar with your notes that a quick glance will tell you the point you are looking for. Do not be a slave to the notes.

▶ Use a watch in your practice so that you know how long it takes to cover the material on each note card.

Speaking from manuscript

If you follow most of the advice in this book and learn to prepare and practice your speeches for extempore delivery, you will not write a full manuscript and thus not have the problems of speaking from one. This is not to say that you will never speak from manuscript or that this method should never be used. The top level executive who must stay within company policy, the government official in high position, the scientist or learned scholar who must be precise, and sometimes the special-occasion speaker who wants to choose language very carefully may need to use a manuscript. But the dangers of poor communication that may result should be avoided as much as possible.

Most people find it difficult to achieve person-to-person contact in speaking from manuscript. President Harry Truman was a poor manuscript reader, lacking directness and warmth, but he achieved excellent rapport with his listeners as soon as he put it aside. Willy Brandt, Chancellor of West Germany, presented a good example of this difference when, after reading a manuscript speech to the National Press Club in Washington in a cold, distant monotone, he answered questions and discussed the same points with great emotion and forthrightness.

The *preparation of the manuscript* is often as much reason for its stiffness and formality as the reading itself. Too often it is simply a prose essay rather than a speech, prepared more for a reader than a listener. It is therefore essential to go through all the steps of good extemporaneous speech preparation, ending up with an outline, before starting to write the manuscript. Only then should it be spoken and recorded as discourse. Manuscripts necessitate more adaptation to a specific audience, more use of personal pronouns, shorter paragraphs, shorter and less complex sentences, simple words, colloquial expressions, more emphasis on transitions and internal summaries, more use of repetition.

In typing the manuscript, the format should be conducive to easy reading, with these suggestions:

▶ Use bold type, preferably caps.

▶ Triple space to make the manuscript more readable.

▶ Sentences should be completed on the page where started, not carried over to the next page.

▶ Main points should show numbers in the left margin so that the speaker may identify them as such if he wishes.

▶ Additional space should be left between main points or paragraphs so that the speaker may insert impromptu remarks. Use wide margins on both sides to allow for this.

▶ Use one side of the paper.

Presenting the manuscript speech involves preparation, practice, and effective reading. Before practicing aloud, read it silently several times, making appropriate markings to underline important points, words, or figures. Also indicate breaks for pauses and places where informal remarks may be inserted.

Practice reading aloud on your feet, preferably with the manuscript on a speaker's stand similar to the one you will use. First become familiar with the content. Then read for meaning, using more variety in rate, emphasis, and inflection where appropriate. Keep trying until your reading becomes as natural as speaking, and become familiar enough with the Introduction to present it without reading. Your objective is to have the animation and variety of an extemporaneous speech. Don't feel that you are merely reading a text. If you have prepared extemporaneously and have written the speech yourself, you will retain an informal manner. As you finish a page, slide it under the others with as little notice as possible.

If *someone else has written a manuscript speech* for you, go through it and analyze how it was prepared, its purpose, main and subpoints, outline, support, and development. Then start to read it and practice reading aloud. Any speech, manuscript or not, must become a part of you and your thought process if it is to be communicated effectively.

Adapting to microphone, radio, and television

Sometimes a *public address system* is necessary to carry a speech to all corners of a large room. However, it is often set up needlessly because some program chairmen think every speaker needs amplification. Where a microphone can be avoided it should not be used. The average speaker, in a room holding up to fifty or one hundred people, may be much better off without a public address system, as long as he uses sufficient projection and enthusiasm. So ignore the "p.a." unless you know it will be necessary. If you do use it, stand with your face about a foot from the microphone. Keep your force and projection normal or a little above, adjusting to the volume level of the system. Stand away from the speaker's stand so that you can speak naturally and with gesture as though the microphone were not there. If you plan to move about or use the blackboard while speaking, try to use a lapel microphone. But above all, keep your communicative directness with your audience.

Radio and television require more adaptations, the chief one being the usual absence of a studio audience. If listeners are present, the radio microphone is like any other, and the speech is to the live audience. The same situation on television adds the major mechanical factors of the camera, monitors, lights, and the like. If you have a live audience, talk to them. If the speech is primarily for the viewing audience, then talk toward the camera with the red light showing. Details can be worked out with the program director and technicians.

One of the major problems of television speaking is the use of notes, for they are very much observed by viewers and should be kept to a minimum. Manner and gesture should not be dramatic but as natural as possible, and extremes of dress should be avoided. The program director can counsel you on any problems.

When any of these media are used, the room and facilities should be checked in advance just as in all speaking situations. It is well to know whether a microphone will be part of the arrangement and to determine whether it is necessary. Similarly check the position of the blackboard, chart easel, and other visual aids if they are to be used.

One of the best examples of the carefully planned and structured use of the television medium was the 1968 presidential election campaign of Richard M. Nixon. The following excerpts from *The Selling of the President 1968* by Joe McGinniss, copyright © 1969 by Joemac, point up the almost chilling way TV can be controlled to present a speaker—be he politician or otherwise—in a particular light:

The TV politician cannot make a speech; he must engage in intimate conversation. He must never press. He should suggest, not state; request, not demand. Nonchalance is the key word. Carefully studied nonchalance.

So this was how they went into it. Trying, with one hand, to build the illusion that Richard Nixon, in addition to his attributes of mind and heart, considered, in the words of Patrick K. Buchanan, a speech writer, "communicating with the people . . . one of the great joys of seeking the Presidency"; while with the other they shielded him, controlled him, and controlled the atmosphere around him. . . .

And it worked. As he moved serenely through his primary campaign, there was new cadence to Richard Nixon's speech and motion; new confidence in his heart. And, a new image of him on the television screen.

TV both reflected and contributed to his strength. Because he was winning he looked like a winner on the screen. Because he was suddenly projecting well on the medium he had feared, he went about his other tasks with assurance. The one fed upon the other, building to an astonishing peak in August as the Republican convention began and he emerged from his regal isolation, traveling to Miami not so much to be nominated as coronated. On live, but controlled, TV.

From a memo from Roger Ailes, producer of the one-hour panel programs, written after the first show:

Mr. Nixon is strong now on television and has good control of the situation.
1. The Look:
A. He looks good on his feet and shooting "in the round" gives dimension to him.

B. Standing adds to his "feel" of confidence and the viewers' "feel" of his confidence.

C. He still uses his arms a little too "predictably" and a little too often, but at this point it is better not to inhibit him.

D. He seems to be comfortable on his feet and even appears graceful and relaxed, i.e., hands on his hips or arms folded occasionally.

E. His eye contact is good with the panelists, but he should play a little more to the home audience via the head-on camera. I would like to talk to him about this.

F. We are still working on lightening up his eyes a bit, but this is not a major problem. . . .

*   *   *

H. Color lights are hot and he has a tendency to perspire, especially along the upper lip. . . .

I. An effort should be made to keep him in the sun occasionally to maintain a fairly constant level of healthy tan.

J. Generally, he has a very "Presidential" look and style—he smiles easily (and looks good doing it). He should continue to make lighter comments once in a while for pacing.

From a memorandum by Ray Price on general strategy from November 28, 1967, through Wisconsin:

Another thing we've got to get across is a sense of human warmth. . . .

Getting across this sense of warmth does *not* require being a backslapper or a "buddy-buddy boy" or a hail-fellow-well-met. . . . It can and should be done subtly, naturally—and this is one of the great advantages of the TV medium (which is a close-up medium) in a relaxed setting, and also of film. Here the warmth *does* come across—in facial expressions, in the inflections of voice, in the thoughtful exposition of a problem *in human terms and in a low-key manner.*

From a memorandum by William Gavin:

We can't win the election of 1968 with the techniques of 1952. We're not only in a television age, but in a television-*conditioned* age—and it's one of unease, of discontent, of frustration, largely undirected or multidirectional, diffuse—as it naturally would be in a suffusing environment. . . .

Humor becomes vital; it cuts through the veils of logic, and shows a human side. It's appealing, democratic, communicative, in the sense of linking the two in a shared experience (i.e., a laugh, which is shared).

Q & A sessions yes; the performance is impressive, and gives a measure of the man.

The question-and-answer period

This frequently included part of the speech situation is thought by many members of the audience to be its most interesting aspect. It may be because the speech was dull, or because the speaker presented the speech stiffly and only became his natural self in the question period. At any rate, this period allows the speaker to enlarge on points, to clarify them, to re-emphasize ideas, to assess the audience's reaction and feedback, and to give the listeners a chance to fully participate in the communication process. We make these suggestions:

▶ The question-and-answer period is for the benefit of the entire group not just the questioner. Therefore, the speaker should address his answer to the group so that it is heard by all.

▶ Unless the room is very small, the question frequently cannot be heard by the group and should be repeated by the chairman or the speaker before the answer is given.

▶ Arrangements should be made with the chairman before the speech starts to determine whether he will be in charge of the question-forum period or turn complete leadership over to the speaker. In a small group, it is better for the speaker to receive and answer questions rather than go through the chairman.

▶ Encourage all to participate and spread the questions around the group rather than have them concentrated in one or a few people.

▶ If there is a lag or failure to ask questions, have ready some areas or points of the talk from which you may suggest that questions be asked.

▶ Audience members should confine their remarks to questions rather than make long speeches themselves, but do not be too restrictive and try to allow brief comments or observations, especially in leading up to a question. Audiences and cultures differ a great deal on this point. In a one-hour question period following a speech in The Netherlands, only five questions were asked and answered because each questioner wanted to come forward as a speaker and speak at least five minutes in leading up to his question.

▶ Answer the question briefly and to the point. Enlarge on the point or supply additional information or opinion as needed. But do not start a chain of talking by going from the point of the question to a series of other points. Be accurate and honest: admit it when you cannot answer.

▶ Unless the situation is very formal, do not require that questions be written out either before the speech or during the forum period as this stifles the kind of free thinking that should prevail.

▶ Analyze each question as to whether it seeks information or indicates a point of view. If the latter, be careful not to antagonize or argue with the questioner so as to offend him or the audience.

▶ It is better to conclude a question-forum period while there are still more questions and enthusiasm and interest are high rather than to let it fizzle out. About twenty minutes is long enough for the average situation; during that time, ten to fifteen questions can probably be answered.

X

LISTENING

A bore is one who is so busy talking about himself that you do not get a chance to talk about yourself.

—*Ed Wynn*

We spend more time listening than in any other form of communication—on average, one and a half times that of speaking, three times that of reading, and five times that of writing.

It is logical that we discuss listening in the chapter following delivery, for it is the other end of the communication process, and all our efforts to become better speakers would be for naught if we did not induce good listening. Another way to look at our development as speakers is to say that every principle discussed in this book is for the purpose of achieving the best possible listener response. Our primary purpose here is to examine our role as listeners, the faults and barriers to be overcome, and suggestions for improvement.

Why listen?

History books are filled with examples of successful men who knew the value of good listening. Socrates amassed his great knowledge by surrounding himself with citizens whom he encouraged to talk while he listened. An acquaintance said of the great industrialist Charles Schwab that listening to him was a rare charm. "Whoever talks to him, no matter what his walk in life, faces a man who hearkens gravely, attentive, eye to eye, until the speaker is quite done." And Mr. Schwab himself once said of speaking ability, "I'll pay more for a man's ability to express himself than for any other quality."

One of the aides to former Mayor Robert Wagner of New York said of him, "He's incredible. He can sit there and give everybody present the impression that the only problem on his mind is *their* problem. And it probably is." Dwight Eisenhower was characterized as a most attentive listener. He would assume a posture of head forward and brow knit while his eyes were focused with intense directness toward the speaker. His military career had taught him the value of listening to anyone on his staff who had information, advice, or counsel that might contribute to an important decision. David Frost's outstanding ability as an interviewer stems primarily from his intensive listening.

Specifically, these are the **values of good listening:**

To the speaker and group. An attentive listener can do much to stimulate the speaker and induce better communication. To prove this to yourself, recall the last time you were talking with a good listener on the other end. He was looking at you intently, compelling you to look right into his eyes as you talked. His eyes and face had a glow of understanding, of sensitive attention to what you were saying. He did not interrupt. He did not allow his glance to wander or allow anything to disturb him. He did not try to read or doodle with a pencil as you talked. In fact, he gave you his undivided attention. And when you were finished he asked questions or commented in such a way that you knew he had listened. Do you remember how impressed you were with this man? A story is told of Franklin Roosevelt interviewing a caller for thirty minutes at the White House. The caller greeted the President by commenting on one of his ship models on his desk, whereupon Mr. Roosevelt talked for most of the thirty minutes about ships and the navy while the caller listened. When his guest had left, Mr. Roosevelt said to his secretary, "That man is one of the best conversationalists I have ever met."

In a group or conference, the attentive listener stands out well and is soon sought by others who make comments toward him. He can stimulate a chain reaction of participation between speakers and listeners, which can lead to total group involvement.

To yourself. The benefits of good listening are many and frequently crucial to the execution of proper work responsibilities and responses that must be based on clear understanding of the spoken message.

We all can look back on situations when, if we had listened, we would have been saved embarrassment and confusion. A friend might ask a small favor which we would have granted if we had only understood better what he wanted. An immediate superior might explain something he wants us to do, but we forget to listen to an important step in the operation. A speaker presents some facts that we would have remembered if we had been listening properly. A son or daughter has accomplished something important and can't wait to tell us about it, but it doesn't take him long to realize we're not listening. Not understanding or listening is one of the chief accusations of the young, hurled at parent and government leader alike. We listen, then:

To be informed. We are constantly seeking information, on the job, in the home, in social situations. The better we listen, the more knowledge we accumulate.

To receive instructions. A primary matter in the work environment, failure to listen can prove costly if we cannot do exactly what is expected of us.

To understand another's opinions or feeling. This objective is difficult because what we are hearing frequently differs from our own point of view.

To appreciate. The sheer pleasure of listening to good music, a play, or a speaker just for entertainment can be heightened through better listening.

To remember and recall. As we listen, we must decide how important it is to store away what we are hearing for future use. How well we have listened will affect our ability to recall and use the information at a later date.

Don't confuse hearing with listening. It is essential to *hear* what is being said as the primary step in the listening process, but hearing is simply the ability to recognize sound. Listening involves perception of the sound (hearing), interpretation of what is heard (decoding), arriving at a decision about it (meaning), and relating what we hear to present and future use (applying).

Faults and barriers

The complexity of the listening process is obvious when we examine the barriers that exist between any two people and the tendency we have to fall into wrong habits. We discussed the barriers to communication in Chapter IV, most of them impinging on good listening. There are also particular faults and barriers that we can directly attribute to the listener. It is interesting to stop and think why we develop these faults. They all seem easy to overcome. Most of them do not deal with the physical or material but are mental and psychological in nature. We are all different in our experiences, prejudices, and habits, and we tend to interpret what we hear in terms of self-interest. And here lies the root of the problem: these barriers are more difficult to overcome because they involve *self-discipline*.

Another basic problem compounds our other weaknesses. Listening is a passive act insofar as specific physical movement is concerned. Speaking requires doing something physical, but we listen while seemingly doing nothing with the body or face. True, we can lean our head forward, look interested, and otherwise try to show that we are listening. But a picture of a man listening is usually like any still picture. Physical alertness helps greatly to induce the proper mental attitudes, but most of what we have to do to be better listeners is concerned with thought process and feelings.

Try to avoid these barriers:

1. *Presuming to listen* or *pseudo listening*. It is very easy to look as though we're listening while our minds and thoughts are elsewhere.

2. *Wrong attitude*. Thinking negatively toward the speaker as a person, toward his subject, or purpose impedes objective listening. Although our attitudes are frequently based on prejudices and feelings we have developed over a long period of time, they may also be induced by more immediate occurrences.

3. *Preoccupation and daydreaming*. We think about other things while the speaker talks, drifting in and out of what we are hearing. Don't make the mistake of believing you can follow and understand what is being said if you hear only parts of it from time to time.

4. *Prejudice*. This fault is likely to be based on emotions rather than logical thinking. We simply don't like the speaker or what he stands for, so we close our minds and refuse to try to understand him.

5. *Stereotype thinking*. Here is the extreme of prejudiced

thinking when we apply certain fixed judgments, conclusions, or concepts that we believe in and accept so strongly that we defy any attempt to change them, even if the facts could show otherwise. Stereotyping includes "allness" thinking such as "teen-agers don't know how to behave," or "current movies are all bad." As soon as we hear something that fits into our stereotype, we shut our minds to any discourse to the contrary.

6. *Wrong assumptions or conclusions.* A variety of faulty thought processes induce us to hear facts that are purely informational, then draw certain inferences from them not intended by the speaker. A speaker may say, "The driver was going sixty miles per hour on a straight turnpike," but we interpret the sentence as, "He was speeding and very reckless." This barrier also can bring wrong assumptions about the speaker himself, which may prejudice us against anything he has to say.

7. *Argumentativeness.* We all like to argue, and as we listen we often begin building a reply to the speaker's point even before he has finished it. Obviously, this precludes our ability to first *understand* the point, because in our preoccupation we probably missed part of it.

8. *Speed.* We have the capacity to listen at a rate about four times faster than one can speak. The average person speaks at a rate of 125–140 words per minute, and it is believed that the mind can receive messages up to 500 words per minute. This being the case, the listener has much "extra" time which he can either use for better listening or for letting his thoughts wander in other directions. If he does not make a positive effort to use the time constructively as a listener, this extra time can be a major barrier.

9. *Busyness.* We all try to do too many things at one time. So we allow all kinds of interruptions to take place while we think we are listening, particularly in two-person situations in an office. We read letters or other documents while the other

person is speaking; we allow the telephone or a secretary to interrupt. In a restaurant or other social setting, we allow our eyes to hop around the room to be sure we don't miss anything instead of giving the other person our undivided attention.

10. *Self-centeredness.* This may be the most basic barrier. In a sense it includes parts of all the rest in that it is what leads to many of the other faults. We have to work hard to transfer our natural tendency to think about "I" or self to the person doing the talking, the "you" from which the message meaning stems.

A program for better listening

Making up your mind to be a better listener is at least half the battle, for in dealing with self-improvement, determining that you want to improve may be more important than specific techniques and suggestions. There is no magic formula for making you a better listener, but we suggest three major areas to work on:

Attitude Tools
Physical Tools
Mental Tools

Attitude Tools. Having a proper attitude is a combination of mood, thought process, feelings, and values. We tend to think positively toward doing things that we evaluate as being important to us. Proper attitude includes the following:

▶ Dispel prejudices and be objective about the speaker and his message.

▶ Plan ahead for the listening experience and consider its potential benefits and values to you before the speech starts.

▶ Make up your mind that you want to get all you can from the speaker. After all, if you are spending your time listening to him, you might as well get as much as you can from the experience.

▶ Open your mind to new ideas.

▶ Project toward the speaker's background, frames of reference, and position.

▶ Regard listening as an active and positive process.

▶ Use the full time for listening, eliminating daydreaming and preoccupation with your own thoughts.

Physical tools are the easiest ones to use for they involve what you do with yourself while listening. But the fault you have to avoid is giving the external appearance of listening while your thoughts are elsewhere. Whispering, carrying on a conversation, slouching in the chair, or even actually dozing off are the worst, most obvious faults and will affect the speaker's attitude and ability to reach you. Instead, you should:

▶ Straighten up and lean forward toward the speaker. The very act of assuming a more alert posture will lead you to be more alert.

▶ Look the speaker squarely in the eye. It may be hard to do if he is guilty of not looking at you or if the room is very large, but directness can help induce a speaker to reach out to you, building a better total relationship.

▶ Your face should show alertness and interest. If the total body is alert and directed toward the speaker, your concentration will improve and you will be able to show the speaker your reactions.

▶ Consider taking notes, but not to the point of excess. Brief note-taking may be valuable, but you can get so absorbed in writing that you are not able to listen for meaning, and you may have to block out certain sentences or points in order to finish recording the preceding point.

► Ask questions when appropriate, either in an informal two-person situation or at the end of a speech. The speaker should give you the opportunity to do this, but try to make such opportunities yourself when questions will help improve mutual understanding.

► Do not interrupt the speaker until he has completed his thought, if in conversation, or the entire speech, if in a speech situation. If you do not agree or have a question, try to remember one key word for each thought until he is finished; then bring them out in logical order. One of the most remarkable instances of the ability to listen was that of Senator Robert Taft during the debate on Lend-Lease in World War II. Taft, making a major address to the Senate, was interrupted by five different speakers and yielded (as is the custom) to each, who then spoke against his position at some length. Taking no notes, Taft arose after his fellow senators had finished and proceeded to respond to every point, weaving them together in a masterful example of clarity, accuracy, and coherence.

Mental tools comprise what you should be doing with your thought process while listening. Your attitude and your physical alertness will have a great deal to do with how clearly you think as you receive information, understand what the speaker is saying, evaluate his points, and try to store and retain them for future use. So just what should be your mental process?

► Listen for exact meaning. Attempt to interpret the speaker's language and diction from the frame of reference he uses.

► Try to determine the exact purpose of his messeage. The speaker should make his purpose clear by stating it directly or inferring it. Frequently, however, he does not; he either fails to state what he is driving at or he is fuzzy about doing so. As a listener, you should actively be trying to clarify and phrase his purpose as he speaks.

► Look for main ideas. Much of what he says may not be important, but his main ideas are. A good speaker will supply these points for you, but often you have to go out of your way to get them. And if he does not present them in a clear or logical order, help construct his outline in your own mind.

► Distinguish facts from inferences and opinions. A purely factual or descriptive statement is not as difficult to interpret as is one that expresses opinion or judgment. There should be no difference of opinion on facts, unless the speaker is inaccurate or does not use a reliable source. But if he is using inferences as opinions and arguments with which you may not agree, you should understand and evaluate them as a listener.

► Analyze the speaker's reasoning process. Is the inference he makes sound? Is it based on facts that can be proved? If a causal relationship is being claimed, look for the attempt to link up cause and effect. If an analogy or comparison is being used, check the accuracy of the conclusions he draws.

► Apply the speaker's points to yourself. Good speakers will attempt to link their points to the interests and usefulness of the listener, but if they do not, a good listener will work with the speaker to bring his experiences and interests into review in relation to the speaker's purpose.

Occasionally you might like to check yourself as a listener, using the following form. And the better you listen, the more you will evaluate and apply good principles of speaking to yourself and thus BECOME A BETTER SPEAKER.

Listener proficiency profile

After listening to a speaker, use this form to analyze how well you listened by placing an X on the line to show your score on each item. Then connect all the X marks down the page to form your Listening Profile.

Speaker: —————————————   Date: ——————————

Speaker and Occasion: ———————————————————

Item	*Good*		*Poor*
1. Did I *plan* for and anticipate the message?		————————————	
2. Did I have a proper *attitude?*		————————————	
3. Was I physically *alert?*		————————————	
4. How well did I *concentrate?*		————————————	
5. Did I avoid *daydreaming?*		————————————	
6. Did I resolve *barriers?*		————————————	
7. Did I dispel *prejudices?*		————————————	
8. Was I *objective?*		————————————	
9. Did I distinguish *facts* from *opinion?*		————————————	
10. Did I *apply* his message to my needs?		————————————	
11. How well do I *understand* the speaker?		————————————	
Can I state his *purpose?*		————————————	
His *main* ideas?		————————————	
12. What was my *total* listening effectiveness?		————————————	

5

Other Speaking and Group Situations

XI

SPECIAL OCCASIONS

It is expected of every good citizen of this metropolis that its mayor should have the fluency of Henry Clay, the solidity of Daniel Webster, and the firmness of Andrew Jackson.

—*Chauncey Depew*

It can be a highly enjoyable—and rewarding—experience to speak at a dinner, ceremony or award presentation, or to serve as toastmaster for such a gathering. The mood is generally relaxed, the audience is often well acquainted, and you can feel they're more receptive to what you have to say. Nevertheless, to be effective these occasions demand the same careful analysis and preparation as for any speech. There are certain characteristics frequently present in such situations:

► The setting may be a luncheon, dinner, or other social event.

► The mood is likely to be convivial, calling for warmth and often humor from the speaker.

► Speeches tend to be brief.

► The chairman or toastmaster tries to establish or reinforce the proper mood.

► Speakers pay particular attention to opening remarks, which should catch the mood of the audience and the occasion by means of common experiences and perhaps humor. Main points should be clear and easy to follow, with fewer points and less formal speech organization. Emotional appeal, imagery, and human interest are more important in development of the speech than logical reasoning. Minimum reliance on notes adds to the speaker's spontaneity and rapport with his audience, whether he is aiming to be solemn or warm and lively.

Special ceremonies

We make these suggestions for speaking responsibilities at special occasions:

Presenting awards or honors. Whatever the reason for the award—an outstanding performance, election to an office, retirement—the remarks of the presenter should tell why the person is being honored, commenting on his accomplishments with a modicum of praise and admiration. The source or origin of the award and its history is usually explained, although the award or gift itself should not be exaggerated, and its value should not be mentioned. If a large award, it should be displayed before the audience. Small gifts should be wrapped. Make the speech fully before calling the recipient forward to receive it so that all attention is ultimately focused on him.

Accepting awards or honors. The receiver may wish to minimize his own accomplishments and give special recognition to colleagues and others who have helped bring the honor to him. He may make reference to the gift itself and indicate his future use of it, opening it if it is wrapped and showing it to the audience. He should try to follow closely the remarks of the presenter and adapt his response to them in whatever way seems appropriate.

Speeches of praise or eulogy. Sometimes the occasion calls for words of praise about an individual without including the presentation of an award or gift. You may be nominating someone for an office, commending an unusual achievement, or speaking at a dedication or anniversary. The speech of praise should refer to the highlights and major accomplishments of the person's career, emphasizing strengths and perhaps mentioning a weakness in appropriate jest; avoid undue flattery and point up the influences this person has had on the lives of others or on the organization. It is best to avoid a strict biographical-historical sequence in such remarks or too formal a speech structure.

The eulogy may be more chronological, but even here it is more effective to single out qualities and areas of a man's life by topics, filling in the dates and events under each.

The nominating speech includes reference to the importance and status of the office, the qualifications considered for it, and the experience and record of the nominee.

Speeches of welcome and response. Brief remarks are sometimes made to welcome a person or group to a particular function, city, or organization. Such persons are usually distinguished in some way, which should be pointed out. Prepare background information about the visitor, find out exactly what role he will play during his stay, and the part of the welcoming group or organization.

The chairman or toastmaster

The chairman at a meeting or the toastmaster at a banquet have similar duties, although the latter's responsibilities are usually confined to the dinner itself. We are including here both the necessary steps in preparing for the occasion and the actual job of presiding.

Preparation will lead to a smoother and more pleasant event for all concerned:

► The program is the most important part of the occasion. It's a simple matter if there is just one featured speaker, though his subject and purpose should be known and he should be advised of the length of his speech. Arrangements should also be made regarding a question-and-answer period, how long it should be, and who should guide it. The speaker should also know at approximately what time he will speak. If an organization is holding a business meeting first, it can be quite embarrassing for the speaker either to sit through the proceedings or await their conclusion outside the meeting room. When there is more than one speaker, the main "attraction" should be last on the program, with others kept brief and few in number. There is little excuse for dragging out a program endlessly at the expense of the main speaker—and a tired audience. The main speaker should be seated immediately to the right of the toastmaster. If other persons at the head table are to be introduced, this should be done briefly. The total theme of the program should have some unity when more than one speaker is involved.

► Sometimes it is well to have a program committee so that arrangements and physical problems can be delegated to it. Too many chairmen try to do everything themselves.

► The physical planning includes selecting a meeting place and room, the table or furniture arrangement, seating positions, and checking on visual aids and other facilities. If it is a small meeting, a conference arrangement in a square, oblong, or T will be best for informality. In a larger setting, normally the speaker and chairman are seated in front of the audience either at floor level or on a raised platform, depending on the size of the room and the number attending. It is always better to have a small room filled than a large one half empty. And it is quite appropriate to ask the audience to move closer together or forward in order to form a more cohesive group. Attention and interest are better maintained when people are seated without empty spaces between them. Arrangements of tables for a dinner can vary considerably, but do try to have as many people as possible seated so that they are looking toward the speaker's table or can easily turn to do so. Diagrams are shown on the next page.

DINNER-BANQUET SEATING ARRANGEMENTS

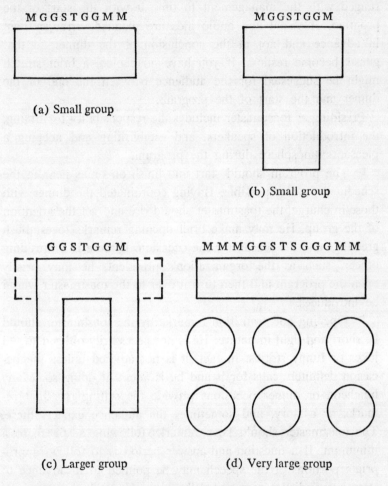

M G G S T G G M M

(a) Small group

M G G S T G G M

(b) Small group

G G S T G G M

(c) Larger group

M M M G G S T S G G G M M

(d) Very large group

T—Toastmaster G—Special guests S—Speaker M—Members or those attending; also would be seated around balance of the table spaces.

SUGGESTIONS

1. Seat according to size of group and room, using arrangement for maximum interaction and view of head table.
2. Place head table and speakers farthest from kitchen serving entrance.

▶ A lectern or speaker's stand, which should be provided for the convenience of the speaker, may be put in place as dinner nears completion. The clearing of dishes should be arranged with the management to time it with the start of the program. If visual and audio aids are planned, arrange them in advance and not at the conclusion of the dinner so that guests become restless. If you have no choice, a brief stretch might be suggested for the audience between the end of the dinner and the start of the program.

Presiding as toastmaster includes the responsibility for timing, the introduction of speakers, and establishing and keeping a pleasant atmosphere during the program.

▶ The program should start and finish on or as near to the scheduled time as possible. Having coordinated the dinner with those in charge, the toastmaster should rise and get the attention of the group. He may make brief opening remarks to establish greetings and the reason for the occasion. If there is a presiding officer, such as the organization's president, he may briefly open the program and then turn it over to the toastmaster whom he introduces.

▶ Opening and transition remarks by the toastmaster should be short and light in nature. He is not necessarily obliged to tell jokes or funny stories; in fact, it is not advised unless the occasion definitely calls for it and he is adept at doing so. Many luncheon or dinner occasions provide the setting for light remarks or a story, and sometimes the audience expects these. The toastmaster should keep remarks following a speech to a minimum. If a question-and-answer period is to follow, appropriate portions of the speech may be pointed to in advance to stimulate audience response. When several speakers are on the program there should be brief transition remarks from one to another, linking them together if appropriate.

Introducing a speaker need not follow an exact pattern, but we make these suggestions:

1. The purpose of the introduction is to have the speaker meet the audience and to have them feel more receptive toward him and his speech.

2. One or two minutes should be time enough and the introducer should never make a speech during the process.

3. Remarks should blend occasion, subject, and speaker.

4. The speaker's background and achievements, particularly as related to his subject, should be mentioned briefly, without a long biographical sketch of his life. Never embarrass the speaker with a drawn-out introduction. It also makes the audience uneasy, for they are waiting to hear the speech, not for you to talk about it.

5. In presenting the speaker, state his full name and the title of the speech. As he comes forward, nod to him and be seated.

The *response to the introduction* by the speaker is normally something like "Thank you, Mr. Chairman" (or his name) followed by a greeting to the audience. Occasionally the speaker feels it appropriate to exchange a comment or two from the toastmaster's introduction, particularly if he knows him personally or if the introduction is highly complimentary. He should be cautious and tactful, keeping humor to a minimum.

The after-dinner speech

This discussion may more aptly be headed "speaking after eating," as there is no such thing as a typical after-dinner speech. The dinner or luncheon is simply another setting where a speech is made, and in today's society it is indeed one of the most common settings. The cliché that "Down goes the dinner and up comes the speech" is almost a way of modern American life. Thus, we have to recognize that many, if not most, of our serious speeches are made following a meal and usually at the same setting. Such speeches may be to persuade, motivate, inspire, or inform, and they would be prepared as would any other speech, though there are some characteristics of the setting that give rise to influencing factors:

► Eating usually puts people in a more relaxed mood. Thus the audience might be more agreeable to points of view contrary to its own.

► Clear and attentive thinking may not come as easily for the audience, making highly technical subjects ones to avoid.

► Relaxation often leads to drowsiness. Therefore, the speaker should include content that can hold the listener's attention. Unduly long speeches should also be avoided.

► The speaker's Introduction should be made warm and close to the audience by reference to the occasion and use of remarks to induce common interest, feelings, and beliefs. Informal rapport can thus be established more easily.

► The speaker's delivery and manner should contribute to the mood by being natural, conversational, pleasant, jovial, and enthusiastic.

Being *entertaining and using humor* in after-dinner speeches is a matter that defies absolute rules and fosters much controversy. If entertainment is itself the thing, the audience does not expect any serious treatment of a subject and probably not a fully constructed speech. Most of us are not entertainers and do not accept such assignments. And if we do make such attempts, we surely should not try to have as our goal keeping the audience in constant laughter.

Entertainment can come with a light and interesting treatment of almost any subject. One can use humor in a variety of ways, such as:

► Poking fun at self, the toastmaster, or the occasion.

► Poking fun at authority or at people in the audience.

▶ Exaggeration, overstatement, or unreality in treating a point or a subject.

▶ Burlesquing and making light of a serious situation.

▶ Incidental remarks, comparisons, or twists of meaning.

Telling stories is probably the most common way to attempt humor. To be good, a story need not provoke laughter; it may be full of human interest and attention factors without necessarily having an amusing climax. Stories are thought to be a natural (or even necessary) part of the Introduction of a speech, especially when speaking at a dinner. This is not so, although they may be very effective in a given situation, if the speaker tells them well. We can make a few suggestions:

1. Do not try to tell a funny story unless you feel comfortable and are quite certain it is appropriate to the situation.

2. The story should not be an end in itself unless the purpose is purely entertainment. It should have a point that allows you either to lead into the speech (when used in the Introduction) or reinforce a previous statement.

3. Try to ease into the story from the speech development rather than say, "Now I'm going to tell a story," or "That reminds me of a story."

4. Know how long the story takes, as sometimes a story can add too much to the length of the speech.

5. Select stories that fit the speech subject, occasion, and audience.

6. Don't explain the point of a story. It should be evident.

7. Tell the story in a pleasant, jovial manner, but don't laugh too much at your own jokes. And don't be too concerned if your audience does not laugh. They have enjoyed it for reasons other than humor.

Briefings and presentations with visual aids

Briefings, usually held for specific people or groups in an organization, are designed to communicate a large amount of information—often of a complex or technical nature—clearly and in a short amount of time.

Such presentations are quite similar to the informative speech in structure and development, with heavy reliance on visual aids. When persuasion is also an objective, main points and support must be couched in terms of values, advantages, and benefits to be derived by accepting or using the speaker's proposal. Consider these characteristics in preparing and making briefings:

1. As the label implies, the total treatment should be concise.

2. The Introduction should also be short and direct, leading to the presentation of main points.

3. Main points should be clearly stated in an initial summary, unless there are controversial points in a persuasive presentation. The organization of the points should be clear, with distinct transitions made from one to another.

4. Developmental material should be selected for greatest clarity and authoritativeness.

5. The speaker should have a large reservoir of information, beyond what is in the presentation, for use in answering questions and enlarging on points when necessary following the briefing.

6. The manner of presentation should be pleasant but serious, with appropriate projection, directness, and emphasis. Too many briefings are given in a stiff, formal manner, with heavy reliance on manuscript. When a presentation becomes a staged perform-

ance, as is often the case when there is too much formality and precise emphasis on visual aids, the listeners are no more moved by the physical presence of the speaker than if they read the same discourse from a printed report. There would be little value in the briefing if this were the case. Although a manuscript may be desirable for accuracy, the extemporaneous method of preparation and presentation is usually more effective. Even if the listeners expect exactness, a good speaker who elects to make an extempore presentation may so surprise and please them that he is extremely successful.

7. Visual aids—whether a blackboard or prepared charts—should be carefully planned and integrated with the speech presentation. The prepared chart will probably be more useful and effective, but some developmental material may be helpful and add informality while speaking. All visual material should be planned so that listeners can clearly see it at all times. If handouts are used, they should be distributed at the proper time during the presentation.

8. Audio visual aids most frequently used for briefings are *slides* and the overhead projector. Modern equipment allows the speaker to control slide use and movement himself, timing the presentation of each with his discussion. He should also try to maintain directness with his audience, facing away from them as little as possible. Any slide used should be worthwhile enough to be given sufficient viewing time.

The *overhead projector* has many advantages in that the speaker can stand facing the audience at all times during its use. It can also be used in a lighted room. The material presented, in the form of data, diagrams, or statements, is made on transparencies that can be easily handled while speaking. And these can be built up by placing one on top of another as the speaker shows a progression of parts that build up to the whole.

Impromptu speaking

We include some suggestions for impromptu speaking because there are many situations, some discussed in this chapter, where one is called on to "say a few words" that have not been prepared in advance. There is no reason to be concerned or falter, particularly after you have become an extemporaneous speaker and are using these principles in your speech preparation. Actually, the impromptu speaker follows the same series of steps in more abbreviated form, somewhat automatically, and in very rapid sequence. As he realizes he is being called upon, he should:

► Accept the opportunity gladly and use his nervous energy for natural enthusiasm and projection.

► Pay close attention to what others have said or are saying and tie in opening remarks as appropriate.

► Plan, by quickly thinking of what the audience will expect, the subject and purpose—usually growing out of the situation at hand.

► Have only one or two main points and determine in what sequence they will be taken up. Jot down a few notes.

► Decide how to develop the point—by explanation, example, story—and whether the objective is to present information or persuade or both.

► Open with reference to others, common ground, and light remarks. State the point to be made. Explain and develop it, then restate it and go on to the next, or conclude while you're ahead.

XII

INFORMAL AND GROUP COMMUNICATION

> Mr. President, permit me to suggest that you consider meeting, on an individual and conversational basis, with members of your Cabinet. Perhaps through such conversations we can gain greater insight into the problems confronting us all, and most important, into the solutions to these problems.
> —*Walter Hickel*

Most of our speaking and listening is done in conversations, interviews, group discussions, conferences, and meetings. And a large part of it, whether social or in business, is informal and somewhat impromptu, with an occasional setting requiring preparation and the accomplishment of a specific objective. Our social environment includes personal conversation in the home, at luncheons and dinners, at gatherings with friends or family, or over a drink. Modern management is trying to duplicate some of these social situations with emphasis on informal contacts to improve relations, inform and instruct, consult, and perhaps make decisions.

It follows of course that all the principles of good speech apply to these more personal situations. You don't have to be making a speech to be aware of the communicative process and its barriers—analyzing the listener and situation at hand; knowing your purpose; being well organized; developing your points effectively; speaking in your best manner; and being a good listener. Or we might put it the other way around and say that perhaps you are "making a speech" every time you open your mouth to say something in conversation or discussion. Hence, why not try to do it well?

We follow many speaking principles automatically in the

countless informal situations demanding good oral communication, once we have adopted them as part of our equipment. But we can go beyond rules and methods. By giving more conscious thought to our conversation and discussion ability, we are able to plan and prepare ahead, determining what we can do to increase our effectiveness in each instance. Whether a conversation or interview with just one other person, a social gathering, or a business conference, these questions would apply:

What is the setting? It may make quite a difference whether you are meeting someone for lunch, having a few friends at your home, going to a home where you have never been before, or attending a conference in the manager's office.

Who is going to be there? And how many people are involved? If a small group or just one other person, your responsibility may be greater than in a larger meeting. And the presence of certain people may influence your participation as well as your bearing and manner.

What is the purpose? It is one thing to anticipate a social gathering where those present simply want to enjoy each other's company, and quite another if certain information is to be explained or a decision is to be made that will affect future policies and operations of your work unit. And you may be expected to contribute some of the information and opinion needed to make the decision.

What will be expected of you? Normally, you are expected by your friends or colleagues to do more than merely lend your presence. Thinking ahead and answering some of these questions before the event will put you in a position to contribute helpfully.

How can I prepare? Specifically try to find out more about the other person(s), do some reading or other research on the probable subjects at hand, analyze the possible sequence of the discussion, and determine some points you want to make.

Conversation

A good conversationalist is one who takes an active and sincere interest in others and what they have to say. It is equally as important that he be a good listener, yet he must always be ready to speak. If you concentrate on what the other person is saying, and if you think of his interests and experiences, you can have a response or question ready at all times. And your reply can lead him to expand, explain, or describe what he is talking about; or possibly transfer his thoughts to your own interests so that you can contribute information or a point of view on the same topic. The key is to be aware of the other person, finding out as much as you can about him in advance. If you have just met him, you can draw him out by leading the conversation into things he will talk about, remembering that *common ground,* common interest, and experience in a subject is all-important.

Don't submerge your own self in the process! You have an obligation to contribute positively in a group, probably more so when with just one other person, and remember that you are just as important a participant as others in the discussion. You don't always have to be a listener. Lively conversation can be stimulating and enriching when you're actively involved. So be ready to bring up something that happened recently or close by.

In your manner, be direct, animated, and lively but not obviously trying to be the life of the party. Avoid distracting people by jingling coins in your pocket or fixing your necktie.

An interesting aspect of conversation in small groups is the tendency to pair off in twos and converse with just one other person rather than the group as a whole. This frequently happens with husbands and wives where the men talk to each other and the wives similarly stay apart. At a dinner table, one tends to talk with the person next to him, still trying to keep one ear on what other pairs or the rest of the group may be talking about to find an opening for joining their conversation. This is quite a natural development, though it usually means you aren't really listening to your own dinner partner. In a small group where everyone likes to know what everyone else is saying, it is often better and more relaxing for the entire group to discuss a matter together, but it takes strong concentration not to drift back into an informal discussion with the person next to you. The host has to be willing to guide a subject and encourage contributions—often very difficult in a social setting.

In the work environment, casual conversation, or what appears to be such, is a major part of the total communication climate. People like to be greeted by their superiors and to exchange information and views. In doing this as a manager of others, one should be sincere and genuinely interested in the other person and not give the obvious appearance of just making the rounds to be sociable.

Tact and conciliation is an important ingredient of all discussion with others, whether it be social conversation, planned interview, or conference. Many of us have a natural tendency to argue and to tune out the other person if he is saying something that does not agree with our own point of view. Although a good argument is useful on some occasions, the urge to win can lead to distasteful and harmful relations. Actually, no one really wins an argument. If you have joined issue with someone on a matter of controversy, remember that *the best way to win an argument is to avoid it*.

This is not to say that healthy differences of opinion are unimportant and should not be aired. Quite the contrary, dissent is the basis of the democratic process and can form an engaging part of discussion and social conversation. It is the manner and the methods used that can make a good exchange of views stimulating and rewarding or uncomfortably tense and even vicious. We make these suggestions:

► First listen and try to understand the point being made. Sift fact from opinion wherever you can, for there is no use arguing over a fact. If you question that what the other person thinks is a fact, or you doubt its accuracy, raise a question pleasantly or supply facts of your own. If an opinion is being expressed, analyze why he is taking this position and the support he uses for it.

► Look for areas of agreement that will minimize the extent of your differences on the point. Don't think of the speaker as an opponent with whom you "completely disagree." Most of the time when we say we disagree it's only with part of what he's saying, at best. And if we eliminate the use of the word, we will come much closer toward conciliating the other person. No one likes to be told that you don't agree with him, for in the very act of saying so you prompt him to think of the full extent that he can disagree with you; hence disagreement grows as each replies to the other.

► Once you have narrowed the extent of differences between you and the speaker, word your reply in such a way as to give some credit to what he has said, such as, "I can see your point of view, especially from where you stand. It might work under certain conditions. But have you looked at it this way . . . ?" If you're going to restate his point, try to do so accurately.

► Once you have established a conciliatory and pleasant atmosphere, you are ready to use your maximum powers of persuasion in advancing your own position in the matter and in making your own points. You should speak with conviction while supporting your position with the best evidence and proof you can muster. In urging the use of tact and conciliation in controversial discussions, we are quite convinced that this will not decrease your ability to "win arguments." On the contrary, you will be a more effective persuader.

We also hasten to point out that *conflict* should not be avoided in conversation. Indeed, it has a positive value in stimulating both persons. Nothing is duller than a cold, indifferent discussion.

This leads us to emphasize the place of *transitions* during a conversation. Both persons should be alert to move from one subject or point to another, particularly when lack of interest or personal embarrassment is evident.

The husband-wife relationship in conversation has received much analysis and comment from experts of every kind. Despite our increased knowledge of rational communication there remains the problem of misunderstandings and emotionalism, which defies the usual premise that if two people know and understand each other they should converse better. To relate closely to each other, tact and conciliation are vital, and one partner needs to be interested in what the other thinks is important. Even if the husband prefers a discussion of the upcoming senatorial primaries to a detailed, and to him monotonous, analysis of which stove to buy, he should try and involve himself in family matters, help resolve them, then lead the conversation into other areas of interest.

Listening is of course essential to the good conversationalist, with this special emphasis: convey in your manner and facial expression your interest in the other person; look him in the eye; be open-minded; raise questions that show you have been trying to understand and have heard what he said; note signs of lagging interest, the desire to switch to another subject, or the need to make an appropriate transition.

Interviews

An interview is *conversation with a purpose*—usually with an intent to accomplish a specific objective. Interviews are usually sought, arranged, and planned by one of the two persons involved; sometimes by both. Most of them are more organized than informal conversation, with an attempt by at least one person to follow a pattern and sequence worked out in advance. There is also a greater concern for time since they usually are held within the work day. The person seeking the interview normally plans and guides it with varying degrees of control, depending on how directive or non-directive he wants to be. In a true interview the tendency is to be more non-directive and draw out the other person. In the case of a job application the applicant will usually defer to a personnel director or manager who controls the nature and length of the interview.

Interview purposes fall into two major categories: to seek or give information, and to persuade, with the latter including the analyzing and solving of a problem and coming to a decision or course of action.

Information seeking interviews include the reporter eliciting facts, experiences, and points of view; the researcher making a survey or conducting a poll; the lawyer getting information from his client; the doctor making a diagnosis of a patient; and the manager receiving a report from a subordinate or staff expert in the organization.

Information giving, of course, includes the reverse, such as a supervisor delegating and explaining an assignment, or any instruction communicated from one person to another in a setting of ample exchange, inquiry, and questioning.

The persuasive interview takes place when one person wants to influence the other's beliefs or actions. The salesman facing a prospect is usually seeking and conducting a persuasive interview, his purpose being to convince the prospect to buy his product. There are countless other situations, such as trying to persuade your superior to adopt a plan you've devised or to raise your pay; or a neighbor trying to convince you to support a fund drive.

In business, the superior-subordinate relationship involves the need to sit down together and discuss work performance. This goal in itself has become an important communicative objective, where supervisors regularly schedule interviews with each employee to analyze and talk over his work. Many firms do written performance appraisals, followed by an interview where strengths and weaknesses of the employee are aired, differences resolved, and conclusions reached. Similarly, the occasional need to discuss a grievance with an employee or to counsel with him can be beneficial if done properly. Today's supervisor should not simply give orders and reprimand his subordinates. He should sit down and get the other person to analyze with him what went wrong. Together, they assemble the facts, explore avenues for improvement, and arrive at a course of action that is reasonably acceptable to both.

Thus, the *pattern of organization* or sequence of planned interviews (as well as group discussions and conferences) tends to fall in or between these categories:

Where the purpose is problem solving or counseling:	*Where the purpose is information exchange:*
Greeting and common ground	Greeting and common ground
Interest aroused	Interest aroused
Purpose stated, sometimes arrived at indirectly	Purpose stated, usually directly
Problem, need, or situation analyzed	Drawing out information (or giving information)
Description and extent	Facts accumulated
Causes and origin	Understanding achieved
Implications and effects	Explanation and description
Possible solutions explored	Checking and verifying
Possible solutions evaluated	Use and application of information

Best solution arrived at   Future action
Mutual agreement sought on   Summary and close
decision or course of action
Close

Questions are obviously one of the chief tools of the interviewer. They should be phrased clearly. They should not be
too broad or vague, and if so, they should be followed with
subquestions narrowing the area of information sought. The
interviewee should easily know whether information or his opinion is wanted and be ready with the expected answer. If it is
desirable to get the other person to respond more fully, the in-
terviwer should avoid questions where a simple yes or no
answer is obvious.

Use *transitions* from one point to another and time them appropriately in terms of the length of the interview.

No matter how well planned, interviews seldom stay within
the time schedule, and for this reason they should be flexible
enough to allow for developments requiring more intense discussion or new attempts to elicit better attitude and cooperation. It is very easy to spend more time than anticipated on a
certain point, and sometimes it is necessary to do so at the expense of concluding on time. A certain amount of control is
necessary if circumstances demand that you finish as scheduled.
In the case of sensitive situations, such as grievance and counseling, an effort should be made to carry over the matter to a
second interview. Control is also a delicate problem involving
judgment, tact, a sense of timing and alertness, and constant
sensitivity to the other person if two-way communication is to be
maintained.

Group discussion

Like conversation, we participate in group discussions in a limitless variety of situations. Mostly we are members of a group, occasionally its chairman or discussion leader. Essentially, the principles of good conversation apply, except that the dynamics of a group make the relationships spiral to an amazing extent, requiring one to be conscious of the presence and impact of every member as an individual and of the group as a whole. To realize the complexity of the total process of *group dynamics,* one may note the many factors that influence communication in the group:

The individual backgrounds and interests of each member.

The status of each member, social or business.

The emotional involvement and feelings of each toward the subject.

The relationship and feelings of each to the others.

The status of the leader in relation to the others.

The leader-group relationship to the subject and the outcome.

The type and amount of participation by each member.

The effect of leadership methods.

The effect of physical setting and immediate happenings.

The major *types of group situations* in which the average person finds himself are social and family gatherings, meetings of an organization—such as a club or professional society—public discussions and forums, committees, and business conferences.

Social and family discussion is, of course, the most informal and defies specific guidelines for planning, organizing, and leading. Most of the time there is no appointed leader, with one or more emerging, depending upon the subject under discussion. All of our suggestions for planning and participating in conversation would apply.

MEETINGS USING PARLIAMENTARY PROCEDURE

These meetings are the most organized and structured, with a chairman who exercises definite leadership functions and responsibilities. Such meetings are conducted with a specific agenda, which tends to restrict freedom of discussion since participation by group members must be in accordance with the correct procedure permitted at the given time. The agenda normally follows this order of business:

1. Call to order
2. Minutes of last meeting
3. Reports of officers and committees
4. Old business
5. New business

Matters taken up by the group for consideration are proposed by motions that are debated or discussed, amended if desired, and voted upon. All decisions are thus reached by vote, and in most cases a majority of those voting is necessary for adoption.

The system of motions in parliamentary meetings is devised to keep matters in organized sequence and to maintain order, to provide equal opportunity to all members for discussion, and to facilitate maximum accomplishment of business. The main motion to bring a matter to the floor and the motions to amend comprise most of the business. Other motions are available, chiefly to provide methods of disposing of the main motion, including the motions to refer to a committee, lay on the table, postpone, and limit debate. A comparatively limited knowledge of the motions should be enough for the average member to be an active participant in such a group. There are many hand-books on parliamentary procedure for guidance of those who wish to learn more and to provide a ready reference at meetings. A table showing essential characteristics of each motion (whether debatable, vote required, need for a second, and rank or priority over other motions) is shown below.

TABLE OF MOTIONS

The motions are listed in order of rank or precedence, with the highest motion on the list having highest rank down to the main motion.

Motion	Vote Required	Debat-able	Amend-able	Needs second	Interrupt Speaker
Privileged motions:					
Fix time of next meeting	Majority	No	Yes	Yes	No
Adjourn	Majority	No	No	Yes	No
Recess	Majority	No	Yes	Yes	No
Question of privilege	Chair decides	No	No	No	Yes
Orders of the day	Chair decides	No	No	No	Yes
Subsidiary motions:					
Lay on table	Majority	No	No	Yes	No
Stop debate (previous question)	⅔	No	No	Yes	No
Limit or extend debate	⅔	No	Yes	Yes	No
Postpone to definite time	Majority	Yes	Yes	Yes	No
Refer to committee	Majority	Yes	Yes	Yes	No
Amend	Majority	Yes	Yes	Yes	No
Postpone indefinitely	Majority	Yes	No	Yes	No
Main motion	Majority	Yes	Yes	Yes	No
Incidental motions:					
Appeal	Majority	Yes	No	Yes	Yes
Division (for vote count)	Chair decides	No	No	No	No
Divide question	Majority	No	Yes	No	No
Withdraw motion	Majority	No	No	No	No
Point of order	Chair decides	No	No	No	Yes
Suspend rules	⅔	No	No	Yes	No
Object to consideration	⅔	No	No	No	Yes
Parliamentary inquiry	Chair decides	No	No	No	Yes
To reopen and bring back business:					
Take from table	Majority	No	No	Yes	No
Reconsider	Majority	Yes	No	Yes	Yes
Rescind or repeal	⅔	Yes	Yes	Yes	No

Public discussions and forums include a variety of settings and arrangements, such as shown on the accompanying page. A group of people may decide to gather to talk over current national or local problems and perhaps formulate action proposals. The question-and-answer period following a speech or panel stimulates public discussion, as does the panel itself.

Most group discussions tend to follow a pattern or sequence similar to the problem-solution (or normal thought process) sequence we discussed for organizing a persuasive speech or a counseling interview. This *discussion outline* is helpful where problem solving or decision making are the objectives:

I. Opening and statement of purpose by leader.
II. Brief remarks calling attention to the problem or situation.
III. Analysis of the problem, its history, nature, scope, causes, and effects.
IV. Drawing out possible solutions for analysis and evaluation.
V. Arriving at best solution.
VI. Determining course of action.
VII. Leader's summary and closing remarks.

Where the entire group addresses itself to the discussion, the leader will try to draw from members as much as is feasible, depending on the time and resources at hand.

The **panel** is one of the best methods for presenting such an analysis to a large group. Usually comprised of four members and a chairman, a true panel discussion does not present speeches by each member. Rather the information, analysis, opinions, and judgments are contributed by an informal exchange among the members, guided by the chairman who leads them through the problem-solving sequence. As a member of such a panel, one should contribute spontaneously and in lively

PANEL AND SYMPOSIUM-FORUM SEATING ARRANGEMENTS

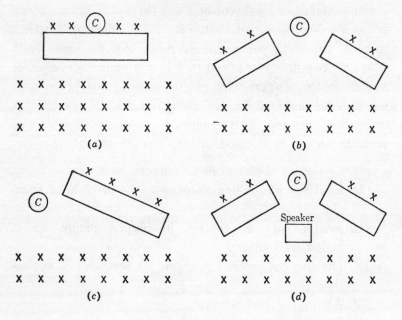

fashion. He should be alert to respond to the remarks of others without being called on by the chairman, and he should pace his contributions so that all get an equal chance to speak. Sometimes a panel engages in a *symposium* arrangement where each of the members makes a short opening speech either seated or coming forward to the speaker's stand, depending on the degree of formality. These remarks are then followed by informal exchange among the panel, prior to the discussion by the larger audience.

The **forum** following a panel or speech involves participation by the total audience in the question-and-answer period, or general discussion if the group is not too large. When asking a question one should be brief and to the point and confine his remarks leading up to the question to a few sentences. And he should not monopolize the group's attention. Our suggestions regarding questions and answers in Chapter IX apply here.

Much group discussion is for the purpose of gathering information as well as solving problems. To give information, members should try to confine their contributions to facts and defer value judgments to the discussion following solutions. **Committees** are established in large part to gather facts and information, such as ascertaining available places for the annual dinner-dance of the club, after which the whole organization makes the decision. Because we are often so pressed for time, both social and business organizations make much use of committees. The average committee is comprised of five persons and a chairman, who guides the discussion informally but does not control or influence decisions. Many committees follow the custom of using parliamentary motions, taking votes and reaching decisions formally to assure group control. If the group is small, this custom need not be followed. The members may gradually reach informal agreement and the chairman observes the trend of the discussion and determines when he thinks a *consensus* has been reached. He summarizes and states the consensus and checks with the group for its accuracy, thus not requiring the members to vote for or against. Consensus tends to imply unity in the group, not unanimity, and no one is officially on record as being against the decision reached. The report of the committee is made to the larger group and is treated by it as a proposal to approve or decide upon, or as a main motion when parliamentary procedure is used.

THE BUSINESS CONFERENCE

The conference is probably the most vital communication tool of modern business, industry, government, and the professions. Large and small, for all kinds of purposes, and in a wide variety of settings, conferences take up as much as half the day of the average manager and executive. Conferences represent the major setting for the practice of participative management, consultation, and recognition, all so important to the individual today. Among the many communicative objectives that can be accomplished in conferences are information gathering, information giving, problem solving, decision making, motivation, persuasion, instruction, and the intangible objectives of participation, cooperation, morale, and teamwork.

Good conferences are usually not accidental. They are the result of careful planning, leading, and participating.

Planning is chiefly the responsibility of the leader and should be carried out systematically, allowing enough time and following these steps:

Determine the purpose. Why are these people being called together? Is it to solve a problem, make a decision, give instructions or information, or a combination of all these? Many conferences have multiple purposes.

Analyze the group. Even though you meet with them regularly, you should try to anticipate their knowledge, interests, and attitudes toward the subjects to be taken up. Who has considerable knowledge? Who believe strongly about the purpose? Are there others who should be invited?

Plan the agenda. List the subjects to be taken up, in what order, the amount of time needed for each. Consider the importance and complexity of the subject and probably group participation.

Notify persons to attend. Each member should receive a copy of the agenda in advance to allow time to prepare, both for the conference and his own work responsibilities. People do not like to be told at the last minute to attend a conference and will usually have a poor attitude as a result. When conferences are held regularly—such as once a week—with the same group, it is well to ask members for suggestions on topics and agenda ahead of time.

Make an outline for leading the conference. The outline is an expansion of the agenda and should be in a form easy to follow, showing major subject areas, questions to be raised, material to be introduced, when to use visual aids, and other details.

Arrange room facilities. Far too often, participants walk into a conference room that has not been cleaned up, table and chairs not arranged, ashtrays not emptied, blackboard or chart easel not clean. There is no excuse for sloppiness, and the leader should know that a neat, pleasant arrangement will contribute greatly to a good conference. Assuming a group of ten or twelve, they should sit face-to-face at an oblong or T-arranged table, or oval or round shape. Diagrams of conference seating arrangements appear on page 176. A pad and pencil should be at each place. Blackboard or chart easel should be set up behind the leader, and any materials to be handed out should be at the leader's position or on a side table.

The participant in a conference should also be thoroughly prepared. He does this by studying the agenda subjects and collecting his thoughts, information, material, judgments, and whatever will help him contribute as a better member. He should think about how other members will regard the subjects and realize the leader's responsibilities for the outcome. Information and opinion from him will help shape the outcome, though he should accept the fact that the decision will be made jointly with the group and may not necessarily please him personally.

CONFERENCE SEATING ARRANGEMENTS

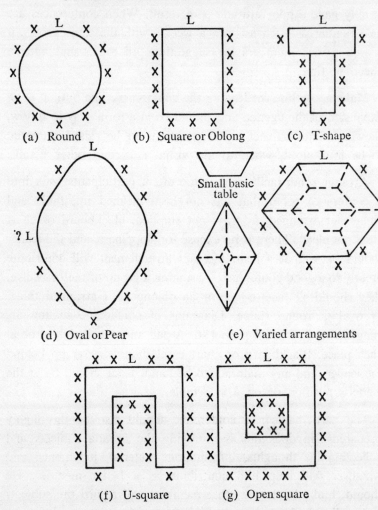

(a) Round   (b) Square or Oblong   (c) T-shape

(d) Oval or Pear   (e) Varied arrangements

Small basic table

(f) U-square   (g) Open square

Leading a conference involves the major functions of guiding, stimulating, and controlling the discussion. Within these the leader should:

START ON TIME.
Keep the purpose in mind at all times.
Be group-centered rather than self-centered.
Establish a pleasant and permissive manner.
Be impartial and listen.
Use questions, transitions, and visual aids as appropriate.
Try to accomplish the conference purpose.
END ON TIME.

► *Guiding* means following the agenda toward accomplishing the total purpose. Most conferences are multi-agenda in that there is more than one subject or problem to be taken up. The first item may deal with imparting information or instruction to the group, which the leader may do himself. He may give a brief presentation followed by questions and discussion. The next item may involve a problem and its solution requiring extensive contributions from the group for problem analysis, fact gathering, suggested solutions and evaluations, and judgments and opinions toward the best decision. The leader must balance his own talking with that of the group.

► *Stimulating* group interest and motivation is the constant responsibility of the leader. He should not try to get equal participation from all group members but should try to get all to contribute while controlling the talkative. Clearly worded questions are his primary tool, along with cases, examples, and visual aids. Again, plan questions in advance so they are clear and specific. They should indicate whether information or opinion is wanted.

► *Controlling* is necessary both from the standpoint of time and achievement of purpose. The time factor will always be a matter of concern, forcing the leader to move from one point to another, and members should realize this. Leaders should be democratic, open-minded, and establish a permissive climate. They should not control by dogmatic statement or by telling the group their opinion on every problem before members have a chance to express their judgments. The leader who tells a group, "I've brought you together to help solve a problem. In my opinion, there is only one way to resolve it, that is to . . . What is your opinion?" will get little or no response from members, and he might as well not have called the conference. On the other hand, participants must realize that the leader usually is responsible for the decision and cannot always accept the consensus of the group. Although he may vitally need group opinion and counsel, additional factors may force his decision in another direction.

One has but to observe the President of the United States to realize that while he must consult with all his staff, he could not possibly make a decision that would follow exactly the advice of each. He must ultimately make it alone. Yet the practice of reaching consensus and arriving at what appears to be the majority judgment of the group is a common one in the conference setting.

Participating in conferences and small groups calls for active involvement:

▶ *Attitude* induces or prohibits good participation. First accept the value of the conference, have a proper regard for the leader and the subjects to be taken up, an understanding and respect of the position other members may take, and open-mindedness in listening to them.

▶ *Planning* by a conference member includes giving thought to the agenda and to each subject on it, including research and reading to become more informed. He may also plan how and when to best introduce his findings during the discussion. If possible solutions are to be suggested, he should think about these in advance, but he should not evaluate or come to definite opinions before the discussion. Even if he participates with fixed judgments, he should be open-minded, willing to change his mind, and work toward a common group opinion or decision.

▶ *When and how much* to participate concerns the timing of remarks during a conference discussion. If one speaks up early, he will be inclined to feel more involved and ready to be a more active participant. He will also be more noticed by the group. Then he should be alert to contribute whenever he has something to say—but not too much at one time. It is better to speak briefly and only on one point at a time, making more separate contributions, than to speak at length any one time. Do not be a chain speaker who starts on a point and goes on from one to another without stopping. *Spontaneous and animated interaction is the goal of good conference discussion.* One needs to be very alert as a listener and follow what others are saying, frequently several others over a period of time, and then speak in response without waiting for the leader. Split-second timing is required. The slow and less-alert person may want to say something but finds himself going all the way through a conference silent because he does not maintain this alertness and readiness to contribute. Good small-group discussion moves across and around the table with little or no leadership but with member responsibility to keep it active and to the point. The leader will step in, point up areas, raise questions, or make summaries as needed.

This kind of group participation is one of the most stimulating and rewarding communication experiences. Conferences will become an even greater part of the effort to accomplish organizational objectives through consultation and teamwork.

SPEAKING AS A TRIBAL RITUAL

John V. Lindsay, Mayor of the City of New York, on speaking of the "affair": "The 'affair' I regrettably have in mind is, inevitably, a four-course, five-hour, six-dais, seven-speaker ordeal for politicians and their power brokers . . . [It] goes according to established custom. Ritual calls for invocations, salutes and tributes to the ceremonial dais-sitters, all of whom are then called 'distinguished.' . . . The ceremonial dais-sitter who is known as 'M.C.' . . . calls upon many other distinguished dignitaries . . . with some liturgical words having special meaning, as follows: 'At this time I want to . . .' or sometimes, 'Now it is my special privilege . . .'

"Each of the chief dignitaries will then address the members for about a half hour or more, each in the same fashion, as deviation from the customary words is not orthodox. Most of the members during this process will sit very still, their chins resting on their chests out of respect for the ceremonial dais-sitter who is speaking."

Reprinted in excerpt from *New York* magazine, 1969

Workbook for Better Speaking

PURPOSE OF THE WORKBOOK

No amount of theorizing, spadework, and morale building really brings it home as abruptly as that moment when you first face your audience. There you are, with your speech all organized, outlined, and practiced—and there *they* are, an audience staring at you and, hopefully, waiting to hear what *you* have to say.

Everyone has the potential—often untapped—to be a good speaker. You are probably far more interesting than you realize, but you may never have had the occasion to sit and think about yourself—about what you want to communicate. Our main objective in this book is getting you to *articulate* your thoughts; to formalize them so you can get up in public and make sense, be *interesting,* and enjoy the whole process.

How you arrive at what you'll say has already been thoroughly discussed, but to make this book as useful and practical as possible, the following workbook includes categories, subjects, and outlines for speeches that should help guide your own speech preparation. We are not attempting to present outlines for every possible speech subject. Nor do we present these outlines as exact prescriptions for particular speeches. If you happen to find one quite close to your own speech subject and purpose, fine. But the chief value of these outlines is to show how a general idea for a speech becomes an organized message.

You will notice that some outlines are longer and in more detail than others. As we pointed out in Chapter VI, outline length depends a great deal on the speaker, as well as on the amount of support and proof he includes. In some outlines we are showing facts, data, and examples in detail. We do this chiefly to show how some of the points can be developed and supported. These materials were current at the time of writing, but may not be accurate or complete at the time of your speech. Obviously, *you will find and use the best current available materials*. In shorter outlines, little or no support materials are shown, as our objective is to show methods of organizing speeches.

First, briefly review the steps in preparing a speech:

SUMMARY OF STEPS IN SPEECH PREPARATION

1. PLANNING

AUDIENCE ANALYSIS
Setting and occasion
Age, sex, occupation, etc.   *What are the communication*
General background   *problems and barriers to*
Immediate interest in subject *consider and resolve?*
Knowledge of subject
Attitude toward purpose
Attitude toward speaker
Ability to learn

SUBJECT
Your knowledge
Your interest
Available sources of information
Appropriateness for audience and occasion
Timeliness
Audience considerations (above)

PURPOSE
General purpose   *What is my communication*
Personal purpose   *goal and purpose?*
Exact purpose
Ability to cover in time available
Relation to your interest
Relation to audience interest and attitude

2. ORGANIZING

MAIN POINTS AND SUBPOINTS
Make random list of all points
Combine, shift, synthesize

Separate points from support material
List main points (about three)
List subpoints under each main point
Make draft of Body outline
List points in best sequence pattern

MAKE OUTLINE (See Forms and principles)

What are the best methods and techniques for accomplishing my communicative purpose?

3. DEVELOPING

SUPPORT FORMS AND METHODS

Facts	Explanation
Examples	Definition
Comparisons or illustrations	Description
Statistics and data	Narration
	Reasoning
Testimony or quotation	
Visual aids	

ATTENTION AND INTEREST FACTORS

Concreteness
Reality
Familiar, closeness
Striking or unusual
Variety
Vividness
Vitality
Humor

4. MOTIVATING

LISTENER MOTIVES AND APPEALS

Tie points to basic emotions and drives
Make appeal to these in persuading
Stimulate the senses through imagery

5. COMMUNICATING

PRACTICE ALOUD AS NEEDED
For learning and confidence
For fluency
For improvement
Use outline—then notes

SPEAK IN A NATURAL COMMUNICATIVE MANNER
Be direct
Be enthusiastic
Use appropriate projection and emphasis
Use natural gestures and variety

SIMPLE SPEECH OUTLINE FORM

The approach to planning and organizing a speech might be done more informally, following this outline form:

My speech purpose is:

The audience is:

INTRODUCTION

I. How I will arouse audience attention and interest:
II. Background or audience motivation on the subject:
   Transition to main points by stating central theme, exact purpose, or initial summary.

BODY

I. My first main point is:
   A.
   B.
II. My second main point is:
   A.
   B.
III. My third main point is:
   A.
   B.
   Etc.

CONCLUSION

I. Future use and application of subject is:
II. Summary and action required is:

SUBJECT CATEGORIES FOR OUTLINES

We have selected these general areas as representative of subjects from which you might be making speeches:

GOVERNMENT AND COMMUNITY AFFAIRS

THE NEW WOMAN

TRAVEL AND TRANSPORTATION

TECHNOLOGY AND SCIENCE

SOCIAL PROBLEMS

LEISURE TIME

ECOLOGY AND PERSONAL WELL-BEING

THE ECONOMY: CORPORATIONS AND BUSINESS

CONTEMPORARY LIFE STYLES

TODAY'S YOUTH

GOVERNMENT AND COMMUNITY AFFAIRS

Broad Subjects

Foreign affairs
  The Middle East
  *U.S.–Russia relations
  Foreign aid
  *Communist influence
  Policing the world
  *Great men
The mail service
Tax reform
*The federal government
Political campaigning
City government
Education
  Trends in education
  The public school system
  *Future of the universities
  *Vocational schools
The welfare system
Housing and slums

* Outlines are developed within these broad subjects.

DEVELOPED OUTLINE

Broad subject: U.S.–Russia relations.

Title: "How Far Can Russia Be Trusted?"

General purpose: To persuade.

Exact purpose: To influence audience beliefs toward not trusting the Russians and to keep ourselves strong.

Possible audience: Chiefly adult groups with serious interests at appropriate settings. Could be given to senior high school and college audiences.

INTRODUCTION

(Attention)   I. Does Russia still want world domination? Does she want peace?

(Questions)   II. Can we trust them in making agreements?
         A. To disarm?
         B. For actions toward peace in the world?

BODY

I. The history of Russian trust in the past is revealing.

(Problem)   A. 1946—conclusion of World War II.
(Examples)
         1. We reduced arms and demobilized.
         2. Russia countered with:
            a. The Berlin blockade.
            b. Continued large armies and armament.
            c. Seizure of Czechoslovakia.
            d. Pressure on Greece and Turkey.
            e. Domination of Balkan countries.
            f. Supported aggression in Korea.

B. 1958—atomic testing.

   1. We instituted voluntary moratorium on nuclear tests in atmosphere and stopped preparing for future tests.

   2. 1961 Russia started series of sophisticated tests for which they had been preparing for years.

C. The Cuban crisis.

   1. 1962 Andrei Gromyko told President Kennedy Russia had not installed offensive missiles in Cuba.

   2. The President had pictures in his desk at the time.

D. Late 1960s.

   1. Russia installed larger ICBMs and Anti Ballistic Missiles.

(Statistics)

     a. These exceed ours considerably. (use statistics)

     b. Has nuclear weapons in space orbit. (use examples)

   2. Her arms budget continues to rise. (use statistics)

   3. The Vietnam war.

     a. Russia major factor in prolonging.

     b. Aid to Hanoi on large scale.

     c. Her ships bring oil, trucks, cement, food unmolested.

   4. Largest submarine fleet grows 12 to 20 more annually.

E. 1970.

   1. Middle East aid to Egypt.

     a. Arms and supplies.

     b. Active participation against Israel.

     c. Helping build more divisions for Egypt.

     d. Subversion in smaller countries. (use examples)

2. Space explorations and objectives are se-
cret; tried to upstage Apollo 11 moon
flight.

3. Constant propaganda against the U.S. in
press and radio.

II. We should continue arms limitation talks and
efforts.

(Solution)   A. But we should be wary and cautious.

B. Success of efforts remain in doubt. (use testimony)

III. We must continue to be strong.

(Action)   A. In arms.

B. In space.

C. In moral courage.

D. In developing best relations with other countries in the world.

CONCLUSION

(Summary)   I. Russia continues to:

A. Have a divided Berlin, Germany, Korea, and
other areas.

B. Support the Middle East crisis and tensions.

C. Build armaments to keep ahead of us.

II. We must not be fooled into trusting Russia.

PARTLY DEVELOPED OUTLINE

Broad subject: Communist influence.
Title: "Is Chile Headed Down the 'Cuban Trail'?"
General purpose: To persuade.
Exact purpose: To convince audience of the dangers in the government of Chile becoming Communist.
Possible audience: Most Americans are aware of and concerned over the dangers of Communist infiltration in the Western Hemisphere, particularly Castro's Cuba. This speech could be given to any youth or adult audience with proper adaptation in the Introduction.

INTRODUCTION

(Attention and Interest)

I. The history of communism in Castro's Cuba is well known.
   A. At first, the revolution did not indicate this.
   B. Kennedy-Khrushchev confrontation.
   C. Current Cuba-Russia ties.
II. But we tend to be apathetic to a new danger in Chile.

BODY

(Problem)

I. Chile was first major country to elect a Marxist-Socialist president.
   A. Salvador Allende elected by popular vote in 1970.
   B. Platform and actions indicate Communist leanings.
      1. Anti-Communist speeches not broadcast.
      2. Press influenced by government: Arrival of Soviet officials and technicians not in papers.
      3. Communists appointed to cabinet posts.

II. People of Chile and other countries show concern.
   A. Chileans' reactions.
      1. Over $87,000,000 withdrawn from banks in one week.
      2. Escudo black-market rates.
      3. Over 14,000 Chileans left country in first 24 days.
      4. Consumers stopped buying.
      5. Farmers delayed planting crops.
   B. Other countries concerned: Argentina, Peru, Bolivia.

III. U. S. Government shows remarkable lack of concern.
   A. Officials sidetrack the subject.
   B. Seem to show acquiescence or nonchalance to the outcome.
      1. Attitudes of State Department speakers.
      2. Political analyst in *Time* (Oct. 19, 1970), "Former U.S. ambassador dismisses talk of a chain reaction as 'ill-informed nonsense.' . . . says U.S. should let them work things out for themselves."

(Solution)

IV. We of course cannot interfere with other countries' government; but we must be alert and not apathetic.
   A. Know the status of their government and present practices.
   B. Follow developments closely and study their effects.
   C. Note relations with Cuba and other Communist-bloc countries.
   D. Urge State Department to be alert and use diplomacy to minimize Soviet and other Communist influences in this hemisphere.

CONCLUSION

I. We do not want to try to police the world.

(Action)   II. Each country must determine its own government and destiny.

III. But we should be concerned, alert, and watch developments.

BRIEF OUTLINE

Broad subject: Great men.
Title: "Winston Churchill's Greatness."
General purpose: To inform.
Exact purpose: To inform of the achievements and contributions of Winston Churchill to the world.
Possible audience: Almost any audience of high school age or older, at appropriate occasion.

INTRODUCTION

I. Men may differ on greatness of leaders of history.
   A. John F. Kennedy measured this as courage in his *Profiles in Courage.*
II. Winston Churchill is universally acclaimed; his greatness affected the entire world.

BODY

I. Known most for his leadership in World War II.
   A. Greatest single influence against Hitler.
   B. The defense of England.
   C. Inspiration and courage.
II. His statesmanship.
   A. Prime Minister of England.
   B. World leader.
   C. Relations with Franklin Roosevelt and others.

III. His personal qualities.
    A. As humanitarian.
    B. As speaker.
    C. As artist.

CONCLUSION

I. We are in his everlasting debt.
II. He set examples for others to follow.

DEVELOPED OUTLINE

Broad subject: The federal government.
Title: "Can Congress Keep Itself Honest?"
General purpose: To persuade.
Exact purpose: To present the quandary of control of Congressional honesty and influence listeners to realize the extent of the problem and be alert for best measures to take.
Possible audience: Adult business or professional groups such as civic, business, and political clubs or organizations.

INTRODUCTION

I. The vast majority of elected representatives are honest.
   A. Occasionally a case of questionable conduct comes to light.
   B. How should these be handled, and by whom?

(Common ground) II. Our concern for this problem is evident by the public interest in such cases.

BODY

I. By what standards should Congressmen be judged?
   A. Same as other citizens?

(Testimony)
1. "Their standards are about what you would find among 535 bank presidents or 535 Rotary Club presidents."—former Rep. Brooks Hays, Arkansas.
2. "You ought to be assumed to be decent, law-abiding, honest citizens."—Rep. Dante Fascell, Florida.

B. Yet Congressmen have official status difficult to regulate.

II. The record of questionable or dishonest acts shows a problem.

(Problem)   A. In total, the vast majority are honest.

(Statistics)
1. Only 22 indicted for serious crimes in 20th century; 14 of these convicted.
2. They do constant favors for constituents, some with risks.

B. There are many individual cases that reach the public eye.

(Examples)
1. Adam Clayton Powell most notorious. (give facts)
2. Sen. Thomas Dodd, Connecticut, censored for mishandling campaign funds.
3. Sen. Russell Long, Louisiana, and Daniel Brewster, Maryland, connected with contractor Victor Frenkil attempt to get extra $5,000,000 for building Rayburn House Office Building. Cases against both were dropped.
4. Sen. George Murphy, California, received $20,000 retainer for public relations work.
5. Congressmen as lawyers represent clients with interests related to committees on which they are influential.
6. They own stocks in companies whose interests come up in new legislation, e.g. Sen. Long's large oil interests and depletion allowances he gets.
7. Even Sen. Dirksen received large fees from clients and had many banking interests.
8. Bankers sit on banking committees and influence legislation. (There are 97 bankers in the House.)

III. Should Congress judge its own honesty?

A. It has made efforts to do so.

1. 400 bills have been introduced, aimed at improving standards.

2. Sen. Case sponsored a bill for complete disclosure of income and gifts, but has not been passed. Many are opposed.

3. Corrupt Practices Act requiring campaign contributions to be listed is violated by many. Senators Goldwater, McGovern, and Cranston reported none in 1968.

B. Ethics Committees in both Houses.

1. House Committee on Standards of Conduct established in 1966.

   a. Chairman Charles Bennett, Florida, considered a "Boy Scout" by many colleagues.

   b. Some members have other committee memberships and interests with corporations. General attitude is easygoing on investigations.

   c. "Official" conduct very hard to identify and distinguish from unofficial conduct.

2. Senate Ethics Committee established in 1964.

   a. Former Sen. Joseph Clark, Pennsylvania, said, "It exists only on paper."

   b. Many attempts to bring charges before it have failed.

   c. Sen. Dodd most famous investigation to date.

IV. The public may be the best judge.

(Solution)
    A. Can reject questionable candidates at the polls.
        1. Rep. Powell defeated in primary in 1970.
        2. Sen. A. W. Robertson, Virginia, defeated in 1966 after doubtful conduct.
        3. Sen. Edward Long, Missouri, rejected by voters while being investigated.
    B. Assn. of the Bar of New York City proposes that Senators and Congressmen refrain from any form of law practice after one term for Senators, three terms for Representatives.
    C. Other professional and business groups should develop similar positions and statements of standards and be alert to exerting pressures where needed.
    D. Every voter should judge what he observes and use his influence at the polls.

CONCLUSION

(Action)
    I. There is some dishonesty in Congress. How much should be done about it? (Make up rest of the Conclusion according to the beliefs and action response desired from the listeners.)

BRIEF OUTLINE

Broad subject: Education.
Title: "Status of Public School Education."
General purpose: To inform.
Exact purpose: To present facts about teachers, pupils, and cost of our elementary and secondary school system.
Possible audience: Parents at PTA or other gathering.

INTRODUCTION

I. Our public school system is a vast enterprise.
   A. 47,000,000 pupils in elementary and secondary schools in 1970; compared to 15,000,000 in 1900.
   B. Total school age population constantly rising.
   C. National Education Association releases annual report.

BODY

I. Teachers
   A. Average age is 39, with 12 years experience.
   B. Total of 2,200,000; 32% are men. Each teacher has average of 23 pupils.
   C. Training: 95% hold college degrees; 30% hold Master's degrees.
   D. Other characteristics.

II. Pupils
   A. Average years of schooling up to 12 in 1970, from 8.6 in 1945.
   B. High school completed by 52%.
   C. Illiteracy down to 2% compared with 11% in 1900.
   D. Other characteristics.

III. Cost.

    A. $32 billion spent per year; average per pupil is $760.

    B. Money comes from local taxes—52%; state government—41%; federal—7%.

CONCLUSION

I. We have much to be thankful for in our educational system. Let's continue to build and prepare for the years ahead.

PARTLY DEVELOPED OUTLINE

Broad subject: Future of the universities.
Title: "Financial Plight of Colleges and Universities."
General purpose: To inform.
Exact purpose: To present information showing the financial difficulties of American colleges.
Possible audience: College students and parents and all mature persons concerned about higher education.

INTRODUCTION

(Statistics)

I. In 1970–71, the total state appropriations for state universities was over $7,003,000,000.
   A. This is big business; does not include private colleges.
   B. Total budgets much more than this.

(Common interest)

II. All sizes and types of institutions are affected by the problem of finding enough money to run them: large, small, private, state.

BODY

I. General economic recession has caused great financial concern to colleges and universities, resulting in:
   A. Less contributions and endowments by alumni and corporations.
   B. Cuts in state and federal appropriations and expenditures.
   C. Difficult for students to pay high tuition and expenses.
   D. Tightening in many ways to cut costs.

II. Both state and private institutions showing deficits.

   A. State appropriations being cut by legislatures.

      1. Michigan ordered 1% cut, amounting to $3 million.

      2. West Virginia ordered 6% cut.

(Examples)   3. Other examples.

   B. Private universities and colleges.

      1. Columbia has $151 million budget 1970–71; deficit of $15 million.

(Statistics)   2. University of Pennsylvania (mostly private and some state supported) state appropriation cut from $12 million to $6 million.

      3. Temple University cut catalogue costs 20%, faculty travel 50%, job freeze on all new positions.

      4. University of California cut construction from $7 million to $2.8 million; dropped summer sessions; curtailed junior colleges.

      5. Stanford reduced yearly budget by $3 million.

      6. Johns Hopkins deficit 1970–71 in arts and sciences of $1.8 million. Cut faculty 10%.

      7. Princeton deficit $1 million in 1970; $2 million in 1971; freeze on staff hiring.

      8. Georgetown deficit $3.5 million in 1970–71.

      9. Harvard School of Education in "dire status" due to federal cutbacks.

     10. University of Chicago imposed faculty freeze.

III. Measures being used to cut expenses include:
  A. Freeze on additions to faculty and staff.
  B. Freeze on salaries; or cuts in some places.
  C. Reduction in courses and curricula.
  D. Less maintenance and janitorial services.
  E. Less new building construction and expansion.
  F. Less research.

CONCLUSION

I. This is an unfortunate trend when higher education should be expanding.
II. We should keep a watchful eye on this problem.

PARTLY DEVELOPED OUTLINE

Broad subject: Vocational schools.
Title: "College Level Vocational Schools."
General purpose: To inform.
Exact purpose: To give information on the growth and status of vocational-technical schools and colleges.
Possible audience: High school seniors and parents.

INTRODUCTION

I. About 20% of American youth graduate from a four-year college.
   A. Has been regarded as the "thing to do."
II. Growing trend toward vocational schools and colleges.
   A. In 1964—about 150,000 students. In 1970 over 2,000,000.
   B. Needs of the 70s point to technical training for jobs.

BODY

I. Vocational-technical colleges are getting more support.
   A. Idea that the only good education is four years of college is now called "snobbish and undemocratic" by National Advisory Council on Vocational Education.
   B. More federal money going to vocational schools.
      1. Federal government spends $14 on universities for every $1 on vocational education. This is changing.

2. U. S. Office of Education indicates substantial increase to improve vocational education.

II. Many states are rapidly expanding facilities.

   A. Oklahoma State Tech, branch of University of Oklahoma, is outstanding example.

     1. Has 3000 students, many in residence.

     2. Draws students from 31 states.

     3. Skills offered in watchmaking, leather, electronics, commercial art, diesel engines—total of 47.

     (Examples and Statistics) 4. About 50% of students were in top half of high school class. About 7% were high school dropouts.

     5. Students make own decisions in choosing specific fields and skills they like.

   B. North Carolina has vocational and technical institutes in community colleges, including some 54 institutions and enrollment growth from 8000 in 1963 to 250,000 in 1970.

   C. Colorado increased enrollment from 18% to 32% in two years.

   D. California, Pennsylvania, Florida are other examples of strong programs.

     1. Penn State emphasized vocational and technical education in Community College Centers and Commonwealth campuses since World War II.

CONCLUSION

I. Should you go to a regular four-year college (or send your son or daughter)?

II. Better consider whether his interests and abilities are in the direction of vocational-technical training.

THE NEW WOMAN

Broad Subjects

*Women's liberation
Working women
   Job discrimination
   The career woman
   Day-care centers
  *Careers at home
   Effects on the family
Sexual freedom
   Moral implications
   Abortion
   The Pill
The feminine image
  *Good grooming
 *Women's fashions
   Personality

* Outlines are developed within these broad subjects.

DEVELOPED OUTLINE

Broad subject: Women's liberation.
Title: "You've Come a Long Way, Sister."
General purpose: To inform.
Exact purpose: To explain some of the goals of the feminist movement.
Possible audience: Men and/or women who want to know more about feminism and its potential impact on our whole way of life.

INTRODUCTION

   I. All over the country small groups of women are meeting to discuss a common problem: their feeling of oppression in a male-controlled society.

  II. This is the core of the women's liberation movement. Its impact on our society cannot be underestimated.

III. To better understand feminism, let's look closely at the movement, its complaints, aims, and achievements.

BODY

I. What is the women's liberation movement?
  A. Purposes.
     1. Bring together women desiring a change in their traditionally subordinate roles.
     2. Make women aware that their frustrations and personal problems are shared by thousands of others.

(Testimony)
3. To quote educator Dr. Richard E. Farson: Women want . . . "freedom from having to choose between marriage and a career. They may want both, simultaneously. They don't want dominance over men. They want access to leadership positions and equal opportunity and equal pay for jobs held by men."
B. Groups within the movement.
1. Many different viewpoints fall under the umbrella of "women's lib."

(Use chart)
2. These are the most important groups. Some are not currently functioning.
a. New York Radical Women. They started the movement.
b. WITCH (Women's International Terrorist Conspiracy from Hell). They infiltrated major corporations.
c. Redstockings. They take the woman's side on all issues.
d. NOW (National Organization for Women).
1). Most moderate, Establishment-oriented.
2). Most members are married, many with children.
e. The Feminists.
1). Stand against marriage.
2). Only one-third of members can be married or living with men.

(Statistic)
f. Radical Feminists.
II. Let's look at some complaints of the feminists.
A. Women have been forced to accept an inferior role.
1. Taught to be passive, submissive.
2. Expected to subordinate her interests to the needs of her husband.

B. Job discrimination runs rampant.

1. Few promotions, chances to earn equal pay.

(Statistic)

2. One-fifth of women with B.A. degrees are secretaries.

C. Women traditionally are tied to housework, child rearing, cooking, and must do these alone even if working.

D. Men regard women as inferior sexual objects.

1. Advertising is geared to being feminine in order to attract men.

2. Men are more concerned with their own gratification than with women's needs.

III. These specific goals have taken shape:

A. Job equality.

B. Abortion reform.

C. Eliminate rigid sex-role definitions.

(Testimony)

1. Says Lucy Komisar, board member of NOW, "The feminist answer is to throw out the whole simplistic division of human characteristics into masculine and feminine, and to insist that there are no real differences between men and women other than those enforced by culture."

2. End clichés like, "Don't worry your pretty little head about such matters." Or, "A smart woman never shows her brains; she allows the man to think himself clever."

D. Change the basic family structure.

1. Share responsibility of child rearing with the husband. Each could work six months out of a year.

2. Establish and maintain 24-hour day-care centers for children.

3. Anthropologist Margaret Mead predicts that by the end of the century child raising will no longer be the exclusive responsibility of the family.

IV. Concrete actions have resulted from their activities.

   A. NOW obtained a federal court ruling barring segregated help-wanted ads in newspapers.

   B. Women's caucuses were organized in the American Political Science, Psychological, and Sociological associations.

   C. Pro-abortion groups have organized to repeal, challenge, or openly defy anti-abortion laws.

   D. A women's caucus exists in the Democratic Policy Council.

CONCLUSION

I. Feminism as a movement appears here to stay.

II. We had all better take it seriously.

III. To again quote Lucy Komisar, "If the 1960s belonged to the blacks, the next ten years are ours."

PARTLY DEVELOPED OUTLINE

Broad subject: Careers at home.
Title: "*You* Can Be a Businesswoman at Home."
General purpose: To inform.
Exact purpose: To explain how to set up a business in your own home.
Possible audience: A gathering of women who are basically home-oriented, i.e. married, with children, and who feel a need to involve themselves in a job or business.

INTRODUCTION

I. Are you restless and bored with your home routine?

II. Do you want to involve yourself in an enterprise other than your children, kitchen, and scouting, but don't want to return to an office full time?

III. Consider starting your own business at home. It may be easier, more enjoyable and rewarding than you can imagine.

IV. Let's look at your situation.

BODY

I. First, how should you begin?
   A. Analyze your skills, qualifications, and financial situation.
   B. Consider your aspirations and goals.
   C. Consult a professional vocational guidance agency.

II. How can you prepare yourself?
   A. Revive your skills with a refresher course.
      1. Some schools offer a free brushup lesson.
      2. Excellent for secretarial, accounting work.
   B. Go back to school and study a new skill.
   C. Bone up at the public library.
   D. Send away for any brochures or materials in your field.

III. Can your town support your business?
   A. Will they buy the product or service you are selling?

B. Do your own market-research survey and find out about your community.
   1. What is the average age? Income?
   2. How many families have children?
   3. How do people dress? Eat? Spend their money?
   4. Are their tastes sophisticated or plain?

IV. What assets do you bring to the business?
   A. Low overhead since you are working at home.
   B. You know your community and have contacts.
   C. You may have inventory or equipment on hand.
      1. If you plan to teach cooking, your kitchen may be well-equipped because you *like* to cook.
      2. Adding machines, typewriters, and files may already be owned.
   D. Most important of all, you have *your* skills.

CONCLUSION

I. You may be better prepared than you think (summarize).
II. Besides the potential of making money at home, you will have the satisfaction of seeing your skills and plans develop while you work in a field you enjoy.

PARTLY DEVELOPED OUTLINE

Broad subject: Good grooming.
Title: "Warm Weather Make-up Tips."
General purpose: To inform.
Exact purpose: To inform by presenting a series of things to do which will insure a well-groomed woman in warm weather.
Possible audience: Chiefly young or career women who must look well all day, or any group of women who should practice detail and care in making themselves attractive.

INTRODUCTION

I. Hard to stay well-groomed in hot weather.
II. Some famous women have endorsed these suggestions, including Betsy Palmer, Barbara Walters, Nancy Dickerson, Wilhelmina, and Lyn Revson.

BODY

I. Make-up.
   A. Use powdered cosmetics, not heavy foundations. Dust on base talcum with sponge dampened in ice water.
   B. Lipstick: Use lip gloss first. Use brighter colors in summer.
   C. Eyes: Use eye shadow after a powder base. Keep with you for refresher.
II. Skin care.
   A. Use freshener or astringent, then lubricate with moisturizer morning and night.
   B. Dust baby talcum powder over entire body.
   C. Apply freshener or astringent after cleansing cream.
   D. Apply alcohol or cologne with alcohol during the day.
   E. Relax in lukewarm bath for 20 minutes. During this, put ice cubes wrapped in cloth over eyes for puffiness.
   F. Use antiperspirant deodorant and feminine deodorant.

III. Hair.
   A. Keep curly hair cut shorter in summer.
   B. Wash several times a week to prevent oiliness.
   C. Use protein setting lotion.
   D. Avoid wigs in hot weather. Use fall or hairpiece in evening if wanted.
IV. Sun tanning.
   A. Sun ages the skin; so not too much.
   B. Use lotion with sun-screening agent.
   C. For excessive burns, use oil.
V. Dress
   A. Prepare for outdoor heat and indoor air conditioning. Use a shawl, or sleeveless dress with jacket, or a suit.
   B. Get porous fabrics such as acetate-nylon blends.
   C. Cotton knits and wool jerseys are appropriate.
   D. Blouse ride-up prevented by fastening large elastic circles (bands) at each side and putting legs through to hold down.
   E. Avoid wrinkled and saggy panty hose. Get with maximum two-way stretch.

CONCLUSION

I. These few simple suggestions can bring ease of mind and attractiveness.
II. Why not try them?

PARTLY DEVELOPED OUTLINE

Broad subject: Women's fashions.
Title: "The Hemline War."
General purpose: To inform.
Exact purpose: To describe the raging controversy over hemlines.
Possible audience: Any gathering of women, for this topic should interest women of all ages, whether working or not.

INTRODUCTION

I. A new battlefield has appeared in fashion.
II. To quote the New York *Times:*
"As far as the fashion establishment is concerned, there is no hemline hassle. The mini, a definition that includes anything above the knee, is out; the midi, an equally elastic definition that descends from the knee to the ankle, is in."
III. But women are refusing to wear the midi.

BODY

I. Why are many women up in arms?
   A. The midi, or mid-calf, length is awkward and unattractive.
   B. Women feel manipulated by stores who are pushing this radical change and holding clinics to train their sales staff in selling midis effectively.
   C. Such a drastic change in apparel is too expensive, for new accessories are also needed, and mini skirts cannot be lengthened.
II. Seventh Avenue manufacturers are blamed.
   A. Many feel it's a conspiracy to stimulate sagging sales.
   B. Few short fashions are shown to store buyers, thus forcing the midi.

C. Says one protester: "They're trying to be fashion dictators, and it won't work."

III. Women are organizing to protest.

    A. Major groups:

        1. POOFF (Preservation of Our Femininity and Finances).

        2. FADD (Fight Against Dictating Designers).

        3. GAMS (Girls Against More Skirt).

    B. Ways of protesting:

        1. Stay away from stores unless they give a fashion choice.

        2. Sign petitions and send them to large stores.

        3. Shop only at small stores not carrying the midi.

CONCLUSION

I. Fashion always sparks controversy, but rarely one so extensive or well-organized.

II. Women are standing up for their rights and refusing to have undesirable fashions forced on them.

III. Will *you* wear the midi?

TRAVEL AND TRANSPORTATION

Broad Subjects

Planning a trip
How to pack a suitcase
"See America First"
Packaged tours
Taking a cruise
*"My trip to . . ."
*Visiting New York City
*Air travel
*The state of the railroads
    Commuter service
    High-speed trains
    Financial condition
 The trucking industry
*Foreign countries
*Bus lines
*Safe driving

* Outlines are developed within these broad subjects.

PARTLY DEVELOPED OUTLINE

Broad subject: "My trip to . . ."
Title: "Visit to an Unusual Place: Gibraltar."
General purpose: To inform.
Exact purpose: To explain and describe a visit to Gibraltar and the unusual nature of the "Rock."
Possible audience: Social or travel-club group of adults. Slides may be used with presentation.

INTRODUCTION

I. All of us have heard of the "Rock of Gibraltar."
II. This is a most unusual place to visit and spend a few days.
   A. Off the coast of Spain; now British; population 25,000.
   B. Founded by the Moors in 711 A.D.

BODY

I. Description of the Rock.
   A. Size is about 3 miles long; three-fourths of a mile wide. Can walk to all places of interest.
   B. Approach from mainland of Spain.
      1. Narrow sandy peninsula connects.
      2. Can use cable car; also see coast of Africa.
   C. Much British influence.
      1. "Bobbies" policemen.
      2. British currency.
II. Living and eating places.
   A. Hotels varied and inexpensive.
      1. The Rock Hotel from $5.50 to $11.20 with bath and balcony.
      2. Others include the Caleta Palace—same rates; Best of Both Worlds—new in 1969—rooms face Mediterranean, with kitchen.

   B. Restaurants and night clubs.
      1. Top of the Rock—very exotic; La Bayuca, the Bahua, Mermaid, St. Michael's Cabin.
      2. International Sporting Club Casino for gambling; Copacabana.
III. Interesting places.
   A. Tower of Homage—fortress built by Moors in 1333.
   B. Fortress tunnel through the Rock called The Galleries.
   C. St. Michael's cave.
   D. Upper Rock: see tailless monkeys and apes.
   E. Fishing areas: can rent boats.

CONCLUSION

  I. Plan a visit to this place.
 II. A memorable adventure.

ONE-POINT OUTLINE

Broad subject: Visiting New York City.
Title: "Enjoy Yourself in New York."
Exact purpose: To inform and describe places for enjoyment in New York.

INTRODUCTION

I. A big city offers much for enjoyment.
II. (develop)

BODY

I. There are endless entertainment places and restaurants in New York.
  A. Theaters.
    1. Midtown and Broadway area.
      a. Examples of theaters and current plays.
      b. Statistics.
    2. Other "Off-Broadway" areas.
      a. Greenwich Village.
      b. Examples.
  B. Concert and opera.
    1. Lincoln Center.
    2. Carnegie Hall and others.
  C. Night clubs.
    1. Uptown area.
    2. Other areas.
  D. Movies. (develop)
  E. Sports. (develop)
  F. Restaurants. (develop)

CONCLUSION

(develop)

DEVELOPED OUTLINE

Broad subject: Air travel.
Title: "The Airlines Today."
General purpose: To inform.
Exact purpose: To inform on the growth and development of airlines and some of their current problems.
Possible audience: Members of a business or civic club at regular luncheon or dinner meeting. Would have considerable interest and some knowledge of subject since most travel by air. Also would be interested in the business and fiscal aspects of the subject from their business and professional backgrounds.

INTRODUCTION

I. Air travel grows more exciting each year.
   A. Space and moon explorations.
   B. Faster, bigger jets, like the Boeing 747.
   C. Most of us fly (in this group), yet less than 15,000,000 Americans have traveled by air.

(Common ground)

II. Problems exist: cost, congestion, waiting, baggage, etc.
III. We should know more about this vast industry. (Make initial summary of main points.)

BODY

I. The total airline industry in 1969 and 1970 shows some interesting figures.
   A. There were 335 new planes delivered at total cost of $2.5 billion.

(Statistics)

      1. Smaller numbers on order, mostly high-capacity jets.

(Prepared
chart)

a. Period 1970–75 finds 312 ordered, valued at $6 billion.

(Testimony)

b. "With continued passenger growth, traffic and capacity will come into better balance."—S. G. Tipton, president of Air Transport Association (ATA).

B. Traffic increased 11% over 1968.

C. Net earnings were $92 million (all airlines), a fall from $276 million in 1968.

D. The rate of return on total investment dropped from 6% in 1968 to 3.7% in 1969.

    1. "The industry rate of return is substantially below the 10.5% set by the Civil Aeronautics Board (CAB) as reasonable."—Mr. Tipton.

E. New airports are being built costing many hundreds of millions.

F. Most major airlines lost millions in 1970.

II. There are problems at airports.

A. Traffic control presents a challenge.

    1. Planes often must wait long periods for landings and take-offs.

    a. Personal examples.

    2. Air congestion causes dangerous conditions.

(Examples)

    a. Over New York City, planes hover over Kennedy, La Guardia, and Newark airports for lengthy periods for landings, and in long lines awaiting take-offs.

    b. Yet the CAB estimates traffic will double by 1975.

B. Washington, D.C. is a major problem area.

    1. Distribution of traffic poor.

(Examples)

    a. In 1969 National Airport handled

10,000,000 passengers; Dulles handled 2,000,000.

(Statistics)
(Prepared
chart)

    b. National handled 225,000 take-offs and landings; Dulles handled 61,000.

    c. By 1980, it is hoped to distribute traffic among 3 airports as follows: National 36%; Dulles 28%; Friendship (Baltimore) 36%.

  2. Dulles presently operates at a loss and often with no traffic, while National is overcrowded and too busy.

III. A major airline: Pan American.

  A. The three largest American airlines are United, TWA, and Pan American, in this order. Russia's Aeroflot may be world's largest.

  B. Extensive operations of Pan American.

    1. Has 165 aircraft.

    2. Operates in 119 cities in 81 countries, with 81,000 route miles.

(Statistics)
(Prepared
chart)

    3. Owns 12 subsidiary companies.

    4. Owns 47 hotels around the world.

    5. First to operate the new huge Boeing 747.

    6. First commercial operation across Pacific—1935, the Atlantic—1939, around the world—1947.

  C. Financial difficulties.

    1. Lost $25 million in 1969.

    2. Stock dropped from 31 to 12. (So have others.)

  D. Service problems.

(Testimony)

    1. Customers complain, "The stewardesses are snappish." "Tickets are not ready when promised." "Their arrogance is fantastic."

2. Rated "Poor" in handling customer complaints by CAB.

E. Management and morale problems.

  1. Too many old executives and directive management.

    a. Founder Juan Trippe recently retired as president.

    b. New and younger men are being hired.

    c. Regional manners are to be given more autonomy.

  2. "Morale is absolutely terrible," says a stewardess. "Nobody seems to care who you are.

IV. Typical regional airline: Ozark.

A. Founded in 1950; serves midwest and southwest.

(Statistics)

B. Flew 15,000,000 passengers through 1950–1969. Growth now is up to 2,000,000 per year.

C. Food service figures in 1969 are interesting.

  1. 740,000 meals served; 62,000 per month.

  2. 40,000 pounds of coffee used; 31,000 cases of soft drinks; 472,000 cocktails served.

CONCLUSION

I. Perhaps air travel will be more interesting as a result of this information.

II. We should appreciate that many problems exist and be patient in seeing them solved.

III. Summarize and look to the future.

DEVELOPED OUTLINE

Broad subject: The state of the railroads.
Title: "Can the Railroads Survive?"
General purpose: To persuade.
Exact purpose: To persuade listeners to favor government subsidy and support of American railroads.
Possible audience: Most adult mixed audiences would be interested in this subject. There would probably be considerable controversy regarding the proposal for government support, and this would have to be analyzed and anticipated to determine amount of support needed and whether to use direct or indirect method.

INTRODUCTION

(Attention
and
Interest)

I. What's happened to American railroads?
   A. At time of increased population.
   B. At time of increased travel and movement of people.
II. Deterioration is evident.
   A. Especially in the east.
   B. Effects of air travel and increased use of cars.
   C. Some western railroads are still holding their own.

BODY

(Problem)

I. American railroads are struggling to survive.
   A. Fewer trains and services.

(Statistics)

     1. 1960 had 1500 intercity trains; 1970 had 450.
     2. Less dining cars and other conveniences.

B. Railroads request to cut back and discontinue trains.

(Examples)
1. Penn Central asked to drop 34 trains; from New York to Missouri and Illinois. Operates 35% of U.S. passenger service.

2. New Haven asked to drop 274 commuter trains.

3. Union Pacific and Northern Pacific asked to drop trains on western routes.

C. Losing money.

(Examples)
1. Penn Central lost $182 million in passenger service in 1969.

2. Government refused loan guaranty of $200 million to pay Penn Central debts in 1970.

3. Other railroads examples.

D. Purposely discourage passengers.

(Examples)
1. Dirty and insufficient coaches.

2. No dining facilities.

3. Rest rooms out of order.

4. Air conditioning not working.

5. Dirty and inconvenient stations.

6. Late and inconvenient schedules.

E. Feeble attempts to improve are made.

1. Washington–New York new trains and faster schedules. On old road beds. Schedules already slower.

2. Other examples.

II. Foreign countries have fine railroads.

(Possible solutions)
A. Japan is outstanding example.

1. New express trains at 120 to 150 miles per hour.

(Examples)
2. New tracks and routes; 3000 miles in next 15 years.

3. Pollution-free electric trains.

(Statistics)

    4. Sleek modern streamliners carried 250,-000,000 passengers from 1964–1970.

    5. Says Yukio Ichijo, managing director of system, the Japanese National Rail-

(Testimony)

    ways—government subsidized, "People laughed at us when we talked about building new lines in this age of jet planes and space. No one is laughing now."

  B. Great Britain system is run by government.

(Examples)

    1. Regards "Rail travel as a responsibility and service to the public."

    2. Was nationalized in 1946. Subsidy is about $140,000,000 a year.

    3. Has fast efficient service: London to Manchester 183 miles in two and one-half hours, at 72 miles per hour.

  C. Other European countries have fine railroads which are government subsidized, including The Netherlands, Switzerland, and France.

III. We should subsidize our railroads in the U.S.

(Solution)

  A. By the federal government, perhaps the Interstate Commerce Commission or other separate new agency could coordinate.

  B. Private ownership might be retained, and private management.

  C. Exact plan could be worked out.

CONCLUSION

(Action
appeal)

I. Use your influence to bring this about.

  A. Write your elected officials.

  B. Develop action groups in clubs and organizations.

(Summary)

II. Our railroads can be a vital part of our future.

PARTLY DEVELOPED OUTLINE

Broad subject: Foreign countries.
Title: "The Netherlands: A Big Small Country."
General purpose: To inform.
Exact purpose: To describe and present information about The Netherlands.
Possible audience: Youth and adult audiences would be interested. Slides may be used if available.

INTRODUCTION

I. We travel to many states and foreign countries.
II. The Netherlands is an amazingly interesting small country with its many places of interest and achievements.

BODY

I. Location and size.
   A. Western Europe.
   B. About 15,000 square miles; size of one of our smaller states.
   C. "Holland" only a part of country heartland, including Amsterdam, Rotterdam, The Hague.
   D. About 13,000,000 people.
II. Dutch heritage.
   A. Water and dikes influence.
      1. Much coastline; about 40% of land reclaimed from sea.
      2. Over 4000 miles of navigable canals and rivers.
      3. Climate is damp and rainy.
   B. The people: warm, friendly; speak English.
   C. Known for dairy and cheese products.

D. Great art, music, and culture.
1. Rembrandt, Rijksmuseum.
2. Ann Frank house.

III. Urban development.
A. Amsterdam most interesting city.
1. Has 50 canals, 500 bridges, many squares.
2. New hotels, modern retail shops with beautiful displays.
3. Entertainment: from restaurants, night clubs, museums, to discothèques and famous red-light district.
B. Rotterdam center completely bombed out in World War II.
1. Has most modern buildings, shops, malls.
C. Other cities: The Hague, Arnhem, Utrecht.

IV. Industry.
A. Cheese well known.
B. China—Delft; Diamond cutting—Amsterdam.
C. Electronics: Philips Company.
D. Van Leer drums and barrels: largest in world.
E. Newest concepts and practices of management; training and development programs very modern.

CONCLUSION

I. You must visit The Netherlands.
II. Even a long stay is not enough to see everything.

PARTLY DEVELOPED OUTLINE

Broad subject: Bus lines.
Title: "What's Happening to City Bus Lines?"
General purpose: To inform.
Exact purpose: To present information about the financial condition of city bus lines and the need for assistance.
Possible audience: Adult groups and civic and business clubs in urban areas.

INTRODUCTION

I. Bus service in cities is facing a major crisis.
   A. About 80% was provided by private bus companies in the past.

(Adapt to local conditions)
   B. Many are not able to continue: fewer riders, increased costs, huge operating deficits.

II. What would you do in (city) if we had no buses?

BODY

I. The decline of bus passengers has been great.
   A. Nation's total decline:
      1. 1945—8 billion passengers.

(Statistics)
      2. 1970—4 billion passengers.
   B. Since 1954, 250 communities have lost bus service.
      1. First in small towns, now in major cities.
      2. Less than 10% of city's population use buses.

II. Many cities have had to take over from private owners.

(Examples)   A. Denver, Portland, Baltimore, Rochester, Dayton, Ft. Worth, etc.
  1. Denver mayor said, "I don't think you'll find a private bus company in the country in three years."
  2. Denver dropped from 1960—40 million riders to 1970—16 million. Has deficit of $1 million a year.
B. Washington, D.C. is largest private service soon to go public.
III. Operation by cities is costly and losing money.
A. Flint, Mich., losing $30,000 to $40,000 a month. Riders declined from 1949—16 million to 1970—1 million.
B. Kansas City lost over $1 million in 1970.
C. Many other examples.
IV. Government subsidy started and will increase.
A. Urban Transit bill passed in 1970, by U. S. Congress.
  1. Provides $3.1 billion for cities to purchase lines.
  2. Does not cover operating coasts.
B. Operating losses will have to be financed.
  1. Probably by federal government.
  2. Local and state funds not sufficient.

CONCLUSION

I. Most are agreed we cannot do without bus systems.
A. One mayor said, "A transit system is as essential to a city as a fire department, police department, or trash-collection service."
(Adapt to local conditions)   II. We are all concerned about the future of bus service in our city.

BRIEF OUTLINE

Broad subject: Safe driving.
Title: "Drive Carefully."
General purpose: To persuade.
Exact purpose: To influence people to drive more carefully.
Possible audience: Any group from teen-agers to older adults.

INTRODUCTION

(Attention and Interest)

I. More people are killed or injured in auto accidents than in all U.S. wars.

A. E. A. Hitchin, Commissioner of Traffic Safety, Pennsylvania, "If drivers were as concerned about the disgraceful slaughter on our highways as people are about death in war, traffic fatalities would be greatly reduced. More people are killed in senseless traffic crashes in this nation than are killed in war."

BODY

(Problem)

I. Problem will get worse as population and road congestion increase.

A. More cars in poor condition.
B. More poor drivers.
C. Less attention to laws and traffic regulations.

II. Speed is a vital factor in safe driving.

A. Speed limits on superhighways get higher and higher.
B. New cars get faster and faster.
C. Pressures of time and complex lives induce speed.

        D. Average person does not have capacity to control high speed.

           1. On a July 4th weekend, "Ten fatalities resulted when the driver lost control while traveling at excessive speeds."

           2. Curves and traveling too fast for specific conditions.

III. Safe driving depends on the actions of each of us.

(Solution)   A. Obey traffic laws.

        B. Use safety features, seat belts, etc.

        C. Keep car inspected and in good repair.

        D. Slow down.

CONCLUSION

(Action)   I. Think about all this as you drive home from this speech.

       II. Drive carefully.

TECHNOLOGY AND SCIENCE

Broad Subjects

Advanced building techniques
The new age of printing
Computers
  History and growth
  Impact on business
  *Types of computers
  How to operate
Supersonic transport
Space exploration
*Probing the ocean
New break-throughs in medicine
*Disposing of waste
Nuclear power
Revolution in electronics
*Production process

* Outlines are developed within these broad subjects.

PARTLY DEVELOPED OUTLINE

Broad subject: Types of computers.
Title: "The Mighty Mini."
General purpose: To inform.
Exact purpose: To present recent developments in computers that make these machines more available for use in small businesses.
Possible audience: A meeting of local merchants sponsored by such organizations as the Chamber of Commerce.

INTRODUCTION

   I. Computers have revolutionized business over the past 20 years.
  II. Until recently, they have been the province of only large corporations.
 III. Now the opportunity is at hand for the small businessman to join the revolution, with the mini computer.

BODY

  I. Why should you be interested in computers at all?
    A. Medium and small businesses have the same problems as large corporations.
      1. The small merchant needs to keep better track of accounts receivable and payable, payroll, and inventory.
      2. Conventional bookkeeping cannot keep pace with growing businesses, and it is expensive to staff.
    B. The retail trade is dealing with a proliferation of products from clothing to foodstuffs and drugs, all requiring close attention.
  II. Big computers present problems.
    A. Small and medium-sized businesses cannot afford them.
      1. These rent for $3000 or more per month and sell for $150,000 up.

    2. Time-sharing, whereby many users share the operation of single large computer, is still too expensive.

B. Large computers are too large, requiring much floor space, air conditioning, electricity, and manpower.

III. Enter the mini computer.

  A. A mini computer can be described as small in size and cost.

    1. It can be bought for less than $15,000, and as low as $2000.

    2. Many models are no bigger than a desk-top typewriter.

  B. Mini computers are relatively easy to use.

    1. They can be readily "programmed" to handle a small businessman's payroll, accounting, and inventory functions.

    2. Small staff required.

  C. Mini computers can be the hub of a time-sharing network, communicating to departments within a small business by means of typewriters or televisionlike display devices.

IV. Mini computers are not just a pipedream.

  A. They are made by over 50 companies.

    1. First model appeared in 1964.

    2. Potential recognized in last few years: now several thousand in use; as many as 50,000 by 1975.

  B. Now used in a variety of businesses, primarily small, although large companies will also make much use of them.

CONCLUSION

I. Mini computers are not a fad; they are a solid addition to the means of processing information.

II. They are ideally suited to small business in size and cost.

PARTLY DEVELOPED OUTLINE

Broad subject: Probing the ocean.
Title: "Mining the Ocean Floor."
General purpose: To inform.
Exact purpose: To present information about a new method for probing and mining for metals on the floor of the ocean.
Possible audience: This should be of interest to most groups because of the unusual nature of the subject, including young mixed groups as well as businessmen.

INTRODUCTION

I. New developments in technology excite all of us.
II. The ocean holds many mysteries now being explored.
III. A new break-through in mining for mineral deposits believed forming from 10 to 20 million years ago.

BODY

I. Deepsea Ventures started this revolutionary technique.
   A. Owned by Tenneco, Inc., a diversified pipe-line, real estate, and shipbuilding complex.
   B. Spent $15 million developing technique in last eight years.
   C. Probed into 3000 feet of water near Norfolk, Virginia.
      1. Long string of 9-inch diameter pipes used.
      2. Operates like a vacuum cleaner.
      3. Lights and closed-circuit television enables seeing the ocean floor.
      4. Draws apple-size lumps of rich metallic ore to surface, along with water and fish.

II. Potential.
   A. Will make into manganese, nickel, cobalt, and copper.
   B. New full-scale mining ship to be built.
   C. Pacific Ocean depths to 15,000 feet have more potential.
III. Difficulties.
   A. Legal rights: Who owns the ocean floor?
      1. Federal governments needs to negotiate international agreements.
      2. Not too much competition for mining rights because of expense and difficult technology involved.
   B. Differences of opinion on value and effect on the metals market.
   C. High cost: to require $150,000,000 in next few years.
   D. Cannot market before 1975.

CONCLUSION

I. Watch for future developments in ocean mining.
II. Perhaps we are only at the beginning.

DEVELOPED OUTLINE

Broad subject: Disposing of waste.
Title: "Recycling Refuse."
General purpose: To persuade.
Exact purpose: To influence audience to press for and support legislation that would financially support technological developments in refuse reclamation.
Possible audience: Community organizations, political and business groups.

INTRODUCTION

(Problem)

I. As a nation, we are being flooded with refuse which affects all of us.

(Attention)

   A. The air and water are being polluted.

   B. Non-returnable bottles replace returnables on supermarket shelves.

   C. Aluminum cans won't rust, are permanent additions to the landscape.

II. Yet technology is available to make refuse useful.

   A. Much of the initiative rests with government.

   B. Our voice is vital.

BODY

I. Recycling of refuse is fundamental to the preservation of our environment.

(Solution)

   A. Less searching for already scarce materials.

   B. Less destruction of the landscape by mines, lumber camps.

C. Recycling is not a new idea.

1. Valuable metals have been recovered.

(Example)

2. Paper provides a good example of recycling.

(Statistics)

   a. It takes about 17 trees to produce a ton of paper.

   b. In 1969, 58.5 million tons of paper were used; 11.5 million tons were recycled. Thus 200 million trees did not have to be cut.

   c. Another 300 million trees could have been saved if the recycle rate were 50%.

(Problem)

II. However, there are serious obstacles in the way of recycling.

A. High cost of collecting and processing means minimum of valuable materials are reusable.

(Statistics)

1. Only 30% of aluminum, 20% of zinc.

2. Less than 10% of textiles, rubber, and glass.

3. Only 20% of paper, the most prevalent waste product.

4. About 50% of copper, lead, zinc are recycled.

B. Companies specializing in recycling are having a difficult time.

(Examples)

1. Houston, Texas, company loses $2 on each ton of garbage processed.

(Statistics)

   a. Can't sell most of material it salvages: only 200 of 1200 tons of paper recycled a day is sold.

   b. Has lost $2 million in three years.

2. Established industries have stake in mining, forestry operations.

(Testimony)

   a. "In the paper industry, a lot of companies are oriented to the trees. If you have a lot of land with trees, you aren't inclined to abandon it."—Assistant manager of St. Regis Paper Company.

C. Regulations, local and national, restrict recycling.

1. Local laws force unsightly refuse-collection companies to inaccessible parts of town.

2. Federal regulations put higher shipping rates on scrap metal and paper.

3. Tax breaks, such as depletion allowances, deter recycling.

D. Final technological break-through is also lacking.

1. "The approach up to now has been totally unimaginative."—Merrill Eisenbud, professor of environmental medicine at New York University and former head of N. Y. City's Environmental Resources Protection Agency.

(Testimony)

2. "All of the exciting things are in technology and all of the answers are in economics."—National Solid Waste Management Association.

3. Paper companies say recycled paper is poor in quality, contaminated by odors, and other faults.

(Solution)   III. But solid advances are being made.

A. Universities are doing research.

(Example)   1. University of Missouri is extracting glass from garbage, crushing it, and using it in paving.

B. The public is getting involved.

1. Several cities have asked for separation of trash.

2. Citizens' cooperation has been good.

        C. Industry is taking steps.

           1. Aluminum can manufacturers paying for return of cans.

           2. Glass bottle manufacturers reconsidering non-returnables.

(Action)   IV. Let's press for further federal and Congressional action.

        A. Must pass present pending legislation: Bills in House and Senate provide $500 million for recycling research to local governments.

        B. New legislation, such as special taxes on manufacturers to add to the costs of disposable consumer products.

        C. Ask government to confine purchases more to recycled materials.

CONCLUSION

(Summary)   I. Refuse recycling is vital to the nation.

        II. The answers are well within our grasp.

(Appeal)   III. We must press both government and business to take a more active role in solving the refuse problem.

BRIEF OUTLINE

Broad subject: Production process.
Title: "How Sugar Is Produced."
General purpose: To inform.
Exact purpose: To explain the steps in the process of producing sugar from cane to finished product.
Possible audience: High school students or adults. Could be given to a mixed-age audience, with proper adaptations.

INTRODUCTION

   I. Sugar is one of our most used foods. All of us like "something sweet."
   II. How does it get from the cane to your table?

BODY*

   I. Extract juices from the cane.
      A.
            (explain details of each step)
      B.
   II. Purify the raw juice.
      A.
            (explain details)
      B.
   III. Evaporate water from juice.
      A.
            (explain details)
      B.

* Outline shows sequence of each major step in process. Details and support to be supplied by speaker.

IV. Crystallize solid sugar from syrup.
  A.
        (explain details)
  B.
V. Sugar comes from refined crystals.

CONCLUSION

I. Summary of steps.

SOCIAL PROBLEMS

Broad Subjects

Slum conditions
    Support the Fresh Air Fund
    Slum clearance programs
Religious prejudice
Minority rights
    Job discrimination
    *Civil liberties
Crime
*Movies and morals
Marital relations
    Mixed marriages
    Divorce
Neglected children
*Drug usage
    Legalizing marijuana
    The urban problem
*Violence
*The Armed forces

* Outlines are developed within these broad subjects.

DETAILED OUTLINE

This outline is made from the famous speech of Martin Luther King, Jr., at the March on Washington for Civil Rights on August 28, 1963. The speech is a model of vivid, metaphorical language and style, replete with appeal to vital basic drives. Several paragraphs are therefore quoted in full. Note also the parallelism of repeated use of the same words in a sequence of sentences, one the speech *title*, "I have a dream . . . ," the other "Let freedom ring . . ." The repetition accomplishes both a rhythm and emphasis of the thought.

What are the general and exact purposes of the speech?

In what kind of audience and occasion could you use this style?

How many vivid words and phrases (imagery) can you pick out?

INTRODUCTION

I. The Emancipation Proclamation set the Negro slaves free 100 years ago.
   A. Today he is still not free.
   B. The manacles of segregation and the chains of discrimination are disappearing.
II. We have come here today to dramatize a shameful condition.
   A. To cash a check or promissory note written to us in the Declaration of Independence. America has defaulted on this note.
   B. "The Negro lives on a lonely island of poverty in the midst of a vast ocean of material prosperity. One hundred years later, the Negro is still languishing in the corners of American society and finds himself in exile in his own land."

BODY

I. There is an urgency to rise from the valley of segregation to the sunlit path of racial justice.
   A. To the solid rock of brotherhood.
   B. The sweltering summer of the Negro's discontent will not pass until there is an invigorating autumn of freedom and equality.
   C. The Negro must be granted his citizenship rights.
II. We must gain our rightful place without doing wrongful deeds.
   A. Not drink from the cup of bitterness.
   B. Keep on high plane of dignity and discipline.
   C. Not degenerate into physical violence.
   D. Meet physical force with soul force.
   E. Must not distrust all whites; many know their destiny is tied with ours.
III. We have suffered many hardships and injustices.
   A. Too many signs "For whites only."
   B. Many cannot vote.
   C. Police brutality.
IV. Let us not wallow in the valley of despair.
   "I have a dream deeply rooted in the American dream . . . that all men are created equal.
   "I have a dream that one day on the red hills of Georgia, sons of former slaves and sons of former slave-owners will be able to sit down together at the table of brotherhood.
   "I have a dream that one day, even the state of Mississippi, a state of sweltering with the heat of injustice, sweltering with the heat of oppression, will be transformed into an oasis of freedom and justice.
   "I have a dream my four children will one day live in a nation where they will not be judged by the color of their skin but by the content of their character. I have a dream today!
   "I have a dream that one day, down in Alabama, with its vicious racists, with its governor having his lips dripping with words of interposition and nullification, that one day, right there

in Alabama, little black boys and black girls will be able to join hands with little white boys and white girls as sisters and brothers. I have a dream today!

"I have a dream that every valley shall be exalted, every hill and mountain shall be made low, the rough places shall be made plain, and the crooked places shall be made straight and the glory of the Lord will be revealed and all flesh shall see it together."

V. This is our hope and faith.

    A. From the mountain of despair, to hear a stone of hope.

    B. From jangling discords to a beautiful symphony of brotherhood.

    C. Work together for the future.

CONCLUSION

I. Let freedom ring.

"So let freedom ring from the prodigious hilltops of New Hampshire.

"Let freedom ring from the mighty mountains of New York.

"Let freedom ring from the heightening Alleghenies of Pennsylvania.

"Let freedom ring from the snow-capped Rockies of Colorado.

"Let freedom ring from the curvaceous slopes of California.

"But not only that.

"Let freedom ring from Stone Mountain of Georgia.

"Let freedom ring from Lookout Mountain of Tennessee.

"Let freedom ring from every hill and molehill of Mississippi, from every mountainside, let freedom ring . . . And in the words of the old Negro spiritual, 'Free at last, free at last; thank God Almighty, we are free at last.'"

CONTROVERSIAL PERSUASION

We have selected the controversial issue of movie censorship to present both sides of a question dealing with persuasion. Using the question as a title for a speech, "Should Movies Be Censored?" we first show a list of arguments (possible main or subpoints) that could be made for or against censorship.

We then show a short speech on each side. Either speech could easily be expanded to greater length by using more examples and in greater detail. Note how main points are introduced and supported in the speeches. To what extent is a direct or indirect method used? How could this be changed or improved, depending on the actual attitudes and beliefs of a particular audience? How could the transitions from point to point be improved and made clearer?

"Should Movies Be Censored?"

FOR

I. Movies can influence moral conduct, especially in the young.
II. There are too many sex movies today, perhaps 75% of all produced.
III. Depiction of sex on the screen debases the true meaning of the sex act.
IV. Sex movies are not true art, thus movies are declining in quality.
V. Violence in movies can induce actual violence in the viewer.
VI. The movie industry's self-imposed censorship does not work.

AGAINST

I. No one is forced to go to a movie; it is his own free choice.
II. Movies do not influence moral conduct, and this cannot be proved.
III. Censorship impinges on freedom of speech and expression.

IV. The movie industry has established a rating code for guidance.

V. Who is to be the censor for others and decide what others should see?

FOR

"Should Movies Be Censored?" or "Movies Should Be Censored"

The trend toward more and more sex, nudity, pornography, and violence in today's movies is symbolized in two articles in *Look* magazine. Four years ago, they ran the title, "After Nudity, What?" The latest issue carries the title, "After Nudity, What Indeed?" The question is being answered in the form of stacks of cans of film depicting the sex act itself in such vivid detail as to leave nothing for the imagination. It is as though we have taken the bedroom from what used to be its warm, cozy, intimate setting and placed it in the Los Angeles Coliseum where the act of copulation can be cheered, analyzed, or booed by an excited mob.

I. The movie industry has practically proved the need for censorship in its own feeble attempt to sweep the problem under the rug by its voluntary rating system. The usually liberal *Village Voice,* says, "The voluntary classification system of films by the Motion Picture Assn. of America is already such a shambles that it will provide additional ammunition for censor groups." They point out that *The Fox* received an R rating (allows children to see it with parents) and yet it "has the edge over most X-rated (no children admitted) movies in delivering the goodies that make censor gatherings such lively affairs."

II. The sex trend has brought a decline in quality which is getting farther away from true art. One writer calls it a "trash explosion." Another warns, "There is now an excess of undressed, oversexed movies which insist that the right to peep is a necessity of art. Too often character is shed with the clothes." Marya Mannes calls attention to the crudity of the sex act as shown by many cheap films and points out that most mature women do not like to see "two bodies thrashing about on a bed." A notorious current movie, *I Am Curious (Yellow),* is called "vile and disgusting . . . a crummy lewd peep-show that deserves to be censored. A recent youth survey shows the reaction of young girls to be against so much depiction of sex, with 66% indicating a need for censorship. Where sex is shown in appropriate taste in a movie with a meaningful message, it is more likely to be accepted as art.

III. The argument that movies influence behavior finds people on both sides, but there is enough evidence of their possible harmful effects to make us pause and take a long look at the problem, especially with regard to violence. Walter Lippman philosophizes that, "Censorship may be clumsy, but a continual exposure to the commercial exploitation of enjoyment of violence is one way to corrode the foundations of a civilized society." Frederick Wertham, noted psychologist, says, "Identification with a character in a movie may be almost overpowering." As *Newsweek* puts it, "Violence begets violence." Even liberal Norway recognized this danger and banned *Bonnie and Clyde* whose theme of violence is well known.

Each of us has a meaning he attaches to a word like censorship. We surely do not mean the kind of control and curtailing of freedom of expression as in Communist and dictator countries. We mean the consideration of standards of quality, art, and appropriateness at each stage: when the movie is planned and produced, when it is being marketed and advertised, and when the public decides whether to see it or not.

IV. One might answer the conclusion that there is a need for some kind of guidance in the movie industry by saying that he (you) is old enough and strong enough to lead his own life and make his own decisions on moral conduct. But even if he is, there are others who may not be, particularly among the young. We have all lived under some kind of parental advice and guidance, and we have enjoyed the protection and rights of laws and social customs. As much as we may like today's free and permissive world, none of us wants to live in a wild, undisciplined society with no restraints whatsoever.

Perhaps the very age group wanting maximum freedom today, the college student, should be the ones to lead the way toward working out a set of principles and codes which give us all what we want in movies but omits that which is too poorly done to be worth our time. This will not be easy. But it might be worth the effort, especially if we think ahead to the next generation (only 1990) and what movies may be like then if trends continue as they are.

AGAINST

"Should Movies Be Censored?" or "Movies Should Not Be Censored"

Today's movie patron can have his pick of a large number of pictures that "tell it like it is" and very much reflect the free, permissive realism of his environment. And that's the way it should be. He can take his choice of *Candy, Inga, Jennifer,* and *Therese and Isabelle* (if he likes girls' names) or *I Am Curious (Yellow), I, A Woman (1 or 2), The Fox,* and *Succubus,* to name a few. All these titles do not necessarily reveal the dominant sex theme, particularly those like *Goodbye Columbus* or *The Killing of Sister George.* And for the college student, *The Graduate* may have started the whole thing. Or for real earthy action of another sort, there's *Bonnie and Clyde,* which is perhaps the leading modern movie using violence as its main theme (with a slight reference to sex).

The percent of today's movies depicting nudity and sex is at an all-time high, perhaps 75%. And why not? This being one of man's most basic and pleasurable desires, why shouldn't he have the opportunity available to him to decide how much or how little of it he wants to see? Most people think this today. A recent student poll indicates that 7 out of 10 students said there should be no restraint.

I. To say that seeing sex or violence on the screen leads to wrong (whatever that is) social behavior is not consistent with actual practice or proof. The Scandinavian countries, where a free no-censorship policy has been practiced for years, have a lower rate of sex crimes than the U.S. Even the legalizing of pornographic literature in Scandinavia resulted in lower sales. One writer explained this by saying, "When nudity is natural and legal, the public suffers less sex hang-ups."

Persons and agencies studying movies and television and social behavior support the conclusion that little or no relationship exists. A leading Juvenile Court judge says, "In three years of study, we have been unable to unearth that first bit of evidence which could be used to indict motion pictures." Lawrence Speiser of the American Civil Liberties Union says, "In the absence of clearly demonstrable proof, there is no basis for the assumption that such a relationship exists." *Newsweek* magazine, commenting on violence in television shows, concluded "There is no scientific data to substantiate the alleged harm of television violence on children." Leading movie directors Nicholson and Arkoff were quoted in the N.Y. *Times,* "Movies do not set patterns of behavior." Jack Valenti, president of Motion Picture Assn. of America, confirms that "Most authorities are reluctant to conclude that the portrayal of violence in pictures results in harmful social behavior."

Actually, many would say that movie themes follow behavior of society and try to depict society as it is rather than lead toward social behavior. One writer (Vincent Candy, N.Y. *Times*) sums it up this way, "I'm somewhat amused at the wringing of hands by various guardians of public morals. They seem to think that movies started the whole mess, when all movies can do really is to . . . reflect what already exists."

II. The legal aspects of censorship reinforce the conclusion that it is not wanted in a free society. And in most instances in recent years, where tried in the courts by way of injunction or otherwise, higher courts have declared censorship unconstitutional. Occasionally a lower court has been induced under pressure of local conservative moralists to ban a certain movie, only to find a definite trend toward higher courts reversing such decisions. The most recent and publicized case in point is that of *I am Curious (Yellow)* which was banned by a trial court, but the U. S. Circuit Court of Appeals reversed this and ruled it could be shown. Similarly, a local court ruled against *Therese and Isabelle* and the Pennsylvania Supreme Court reversed this decision with this strong statement by Judge

H. X. O'Brien, "It was a shocking breach of justice to enjoin this film."

U. S. Supreme Court Justices have been very emphatic with such statements as these against censorship: Justice Douglas, "Censorship of movies is unconstitutional because it is a prior restraint and violation of the First Amendment." Justice Brennan, "Motion pictures are within the ambit of the constitutional guarantees of freedom of speech and the press."

III. The movie industry itself has taken a major step against the need for censorship by classifying movies and advising the public what to expect. Its self-rating system has been described by the *Hollywood Reporter* as "the sanest, most rational plan yet devised to provide safeguards: 1) to assure the freedom of the screen without government intervention; and 2) to inform parents about the content of a film and restrict children from certain movies. This voluntary system should be a boon to creative freedom of the screen."

IV. Perhaps the strongest argument against censorship can be made in raising the question, *who* is to be the censor? Why should one person or a group make a subjective judgment that restricts the freedom of others to do and choose as they wish? Who is to say what degree and kind of "expertise" is necessary to make such judgment and become the regulator of other people's social and moral behavior?

Freedom of speech and expression is the right of every individual in a free society, and movies are a part of this freedom. No one forces us to go to them and no one should tell us which ones to stay away from. The right to create them and the right to see them must remain free.

ONE-POINT SPEECH OUTLINE

Broad Subject: Drug usage.
Title: "Sniffing—a Dangerous Drug Habit."
Exact purpose: To persuade against the practice of sniffing.

INTRODUCTION

I. Sniffing as a drug habit first noticed in California in late 1950s.
II. Has spread to alarmingly increasing proportions.

BODY

I. Sniffing chemical solvents is very harmful to health.
  A. Plastic bag use decreases oxygen and subject rebreathes carbon monoxide, along with other chemicals.
  B. May cause death.
    1. 110 American youths, age 11–23, died in last ten years.
    2. 81 of these from suburban middle-income white families.
    3. Death due to brain damage and respiratory failure.
    4. Dr. Millard Bass, Johns Hopkins University, "A rapidly rising number of solvent sniffers are dying suddenly and unexpectedly."
  C. Solvents used include airplane glue, spot removers, gasoline, certain aerosol cans, and others.
  D. Examples are striking.
    1. One 17-year-old boy in back seat of friends car, "I think my heart is stopping." Died in the car.
    2. Other examples.

CONCLUSION

(develop)

PARTLY DEVELOPED OUTLINE

Broad subject: Violence.
Title: "Violence in the U.S."
General purpose: To persuade.
Exact purpose: To persuade listeners to be alert to the problem of violence in our country and to take steps to control this.
Possible audience: Adult group or college students.

INTRODUCTION

(Attention)   I. U.S. has been experiencing extremes of violence.
(Common   II. Yet all of us want a peaceful society.
ground)

BODY

     I. Use of violence evident throughout the country.
(Problem)   A. Riots in major cities.
       1. Los Angeles.
(Examples)   2. Detroit.
       3. Washington.
       4. Urban guerrilla warfare.
     B. Campus unrest: examples are limitless.
       1. Kent State, Jackson State.
       2. California, Penn State, Ohio State, Wisconsin.
       3. Ivy League: Columbia, Yale, Princeton.
     C. By particular groups.
       1. Black Panthers.
       2. SDS.
       3. Tate murders and others.

D. Bombing of buildings in cities.
   1. New York.
   2. Other examples.

II. We must determine cause and analyze conditions.

(Solution)
A. Race discrimination.
B. Poverty, want, unemployment.
C. Social changes and unrest.
D. Vietnam war.

III. We must continue to find solutions and improve conditions.

(Action)
A. Correct social inequalities.
B. End the Vietnam war.
C. Economic factors.
D. Education.
E. Government attitude and policies.
F. Strong police action where necessary.

CONCLUSION

I. All of us can help in our own attitudes and actions.
II. Lend support where needed.

BRIEF OUTLINE

Broad subject: The Armed forces.
Title: "Join the Army Reserves."
General purpose: To persuade.
Exact purpose: To persuade audience to think favorably of the Army Reserves and to consider joining.
Possible audience: Mature men who have probably already fulfilled their military responsibilities or are past the draft age.

INTRODUCTION

(Attention and Need)

I. There will always be a need for a strong military establishment.

II. Did you ever stop to realize how you can help fill this need with many rewards to yourself?

BODY

I. The Army Reserves.

(Solution)

  A. What it is.

  B. What it does.

II. Benefits to you as Army Reserve member.

  A. Pay.

  B. Technical training and schooling.

  C. Valuable contacts and associates.

  D. Leadership opportunities.

  E. Retirement pension.

  F. Patriotic satisfaction.

III. Benefits to country.

(Appeal)

  A. Help protect U.S.

  B. Protect future generations.

  C. Protect freedom and liberties.

CONCLUSION

I. Sum up benefits.

(Action) II. Why not give this serious thought, become a "Citizen Soldier," and add new dimensions to your life?

LEISURE TIME

Broad Subjects

Reading for pleasure
Learning to paint
The arts
  The state of the theater
  The high cost of opera
 *The quality of television
*Building an art collection
*Unusual living
Sports
  How to play . . .
  How to watch a football game
  The Davis Cup matches
 *The All-Star baseball team
  Training for the Olympics
Life in a retirement community
*Resorts

* Outlines are developed within these broad subjects.

PARTLY DEVELOPED OUTLINE

Broad subject: The quality of television.
Title: "What's Wrong with Children's Television?"
General purpose: To persuade.
Exact purpose: To convince an audience that there are not enough female-oriented children's shows with believable heroines.
Possible audience: Any adult group—particularly of parents—with an interest in the future of television.

INTRODUCTION

I. Amid all analysis of children's television, one key factor is being overlooked: Programs, from the simplest cartoons to "Sesame Street," are remarkably male-oriented.

II. The little-girl image is still Little Miss Muffet and Olive Oyl. Equal billing for the heroine is rare.

III. Anyone interested in women's rights and the future of television should listen closely to these facts.

BODY

I. Little girls face discrimination at an early age.
   A. Most cartoons don't bother to acknowledge the existence of a second sex, and those that do just have females as girl friends or mothers.
   B. Little girls grow up with the stereotype of being less than equal.

II. Cartoon heroines simper, faint, or gaze adoringly at the hero.
   A. Examples.
   B. Exception.

III. Live action shows are no better.
   A. Even Lassie is a male.

B. "Captain Kangaroo" is all male—including the Dancing Bear.

C. Susan on "Sesame Street" is usually seen in the kitchen.

IV. Commercials for children, especially when energy and vigor are being shown, feature boys.

    A. Examples.

    B. Exception—helping to bathe the baby or cook.

CONCLUSION

I. Summarize the problem.

II. Discuss what can be done.

    A. Write letters.

    B. Boycott sponsoring products.

    C. Control what your child watches.

PARTLY DEVELOPED OUTLINE

Broad subject: Building an art collection.
Title: "The Print Explosion."
General purpose: To inform.
Exact purpose: To inform about the growing interest in collecting prints, their value, and considerations in purchasing them.
Possible audience: A club or organization in the general field of art, or an adult audience with sufficient education or maturity and economic means to purchase art for the home or as a collector.

INTRODUCTION

(Quotation)

I. "It is now a status symbol to have a collection of fine prints," says one authority.
   A. Many Americans are turning to collecting prints; partly because of the high price of paintings.
   B. Prints are etchings, engravings, and lithographs.

II. This information should help you in assessing prints and buying them.

BODY

(Examples)

I. Values have risen markedly in recent years.
   A. Some examples will show this.
      1. A Matisse lithograph in 1960 was worth $350; 1970 worth $5000.
      2. Old Master prints multiplied 37 times in value since 1950.
      3. A Rembrandt etching increased in value from $40,000 to $77,000.

(Statistics)

    4. A Mary Cassatt in 1960 was $150; 1970 worth $4500.

    5. Picasso's "After Cranach" in 1960 was $600; 1970 worth $35,000.

  B. Must be originals.

    1. There are many reproductions and fake signatures.

    2. High-pressure auctioneers try to sell unknown artists.

II. Purchasing prints requires care and caution.

  A. Follow these suggestions to be sure of originals.

    1. Check catalogues and art books.

    2. Visit museum print cabinets.

    3. Browse in galleries and shops.

    4. Buy from established print dealers.

    5. Avoid one-shot print exhibitions and auctions unless checked first.

    6. Avoid "bargains."

    7. Look out for "restrikes" or rerun of original plates.

    8. Avoid hottest print fads and stick to traditional.

(Authority)

  B. Invest for profit. Explore the following categories recommended by Sylvan Cole, president of Associated American Artists and largest print dealer in the U.S.

(Examples)

    1. French 19th century artists such as Baptiste, Corot, Millet, and Appiani. Some can be bought for $20 to $200; others up to $600.

    2. American early 20th century artists such as Benton, Curry, Wood, and Sloan. Average about $150 to $750.

    3. British: Cameron, Bone, McBey are low

priced and "Are beginning to inch up," says Cole.

4. Print makers of the 15th, 16th, and 17th centuries are not known but may be good buys at less than $100.

5. Observe that a great oil painter or sculptor may not be a good print maker.

6. Rarity or scarcity will bring price up.

CONCLUSION

I. Remember these suggestions in shopping for prints. (summarize)

II. Maybe "The Print Explosion" can be part of your future.

PARTLY DEVELOPED OUTLINE

Broad subject: Unusual living.
Title: "Houseboats: A New Living Experience."
General purpose: To inform.
Exact purpose: To acquaint listeners with houseboats as a means for vacationing or as a home.
Possible audience: Adult husband and wife groups of middle class would be interested; also family groups with children old enough to appreciate this subject.

INTRODUCTION

I. Why not try something new for your next vacation?
II. Houseboats are becoming increasingly popular and available.
    A. There are 100 marinas between Staten Island and Troy, N.Y., where these and other boats can be kept.
    B. "Women like them," says one dealer.

BODY

I. There are many types and sizes.
    A. Range from 20 to 60 feet in length; average about 40 feet.
    B. Accommodations include galley for cooking, berths for sleeping.
        1. Large boats have separate bedrooms and bath.
    C. There are condominiums with pier and strip of land.
        1. 45 feet sells for about $45,000.
        2. Can rent (sublet) out to others when not using.
    D. Houseboat hotels are becoming available.
        1. Yugoslavia has chain with five ports available.
        2. Being planned in Spain, Mexico, and the Bahamas.

II. Renting a houseboat.
 A. A 30- to 50-foot boat fully equipped runs $300 up per week.
 B. In N.Y. area, older boats may be rented for much less. (use examples)
III. Living on a houseboat.
 A. Can be relaxing and in pleasant scenic surroundings.
  1. If tired of one place, move to another.
  2. "It's very private, like living in the country," says one husband at City Island, Bronx, N.Y., location.
  3. At Stony Point, N.Y., a proprietor says, "The air is invigorating and good to breathe."
  4. A doctor and family live in a houseboat at 79th Street Boat Basin in New York City where the rent is low.
 B. Moving from place to place.
  1. New scenery and environment.
  2. Can travel about 15 to 20 knots per hour and move an average of 100 miles a day if desired.
  3. Does not roll as much as other boats, due to broad bottom.

CONCLUSION

 I. Look into this unusual way of living.
 II. Consider a week's trial for your next vacation.

PARTLY DEVELOPED OUTLINE

Broad subject: The All-Star baseball team.
Title: "Who Should Pick the All-Star Team?"
General purpose: To inform and get audience reaction to decision.
Exact purpose: To inform audience about methods for selecting the All-Star baseball team and arrive at audience decision for best method by discussion after the speech.
Possible audience: This would be appropriate for mixed audiences of all age levels but primarily for men and boys at occasions where sports, and baseball in particular, would be of interest.

INTRODUCTION

    I. The All-Star baseball game is a major highlight of the sport season.

    II. Who should select the players who made up the teams?

BODY

I. History.
    A. Fans selected players by ballot until 1957.
        1. In 1957, ballot boxes were "stuffed" in Cincinnati.
        2. Some people voted 200 times for home players.
    B. Players selected the teams from 1958 to 1970.
        1. Worked fairly smoothly.
        2. Starting teams selected by player ballot.
        3. Managers pick pitchers and others.

C. Many fans felt they should be the ones to vote for the team.

II. In 1970, fans again were given selection.

  A. Teams expanded to 24; ballot boxes set up in each park and in 75,000 retail stores.

    1. Printed 20,000,000 ballots.

    2. Paid for by Gillette Company.

  B. Computers needed to count ballots.

    1. Computers cards limited to 48 names of players in each league. With 12 teams, this meant only four players from each team could be shown on ballots.

    2. How select these names? Were nominated by commissioner's office in February, with help of 24 player representatives and 24 managers.

    3. Problem of what names should be nominated in February for game to be played in July. Who would be outstanding then?

  C. This system led to:

    1. Including players who were idle or injured early part of the season. (use examples)

    2. Excluding 10 of the 20 top hitters in July. (use examples)

    3. Excluding players with phenomenal records up to July.

III. Which system do you think works best? Is most fair?

  A. Players selecting the team.

    1. Advantages.

    2. Disadvantages.

  B. Fans selecting the team.

    1. Advantages.

    2. Disadvantages.

CONCLUSION

**(Audience
discussion)**

I. Here, then, is the picture of each method.

II. Let's discuss this and see what our combined judgment is for the best method of selection. Maybe we can arrive at a better method or improve on whichever one of these we think is best.

BRIEF OUTLINE

Broad subject: Resorts.
Title: "Out-of-the-Way Resorts."
General purpose: To inform.
Exact purpose: To present information on resorts and unusual places
   in the U.S. that are little known and off the beaten track.
Possible audience: Adult groups at appropriate occasion for subject.

INTRODUCTION

I. Tendency to go to big well-known resorts for vacation trips.
II. Why not try something new, unusual, and less expensive?

BODY

I. American hideaways.
   A. New England small towns.
   B. New Mexico old Spanish towns.
   C. Gold Rush towns of California.
II. Islands.
   A. European atmosphere.
      1. Beaver Island, Mich.
      2. Isle of Orleans, Quebec.
      3. Washington Island, Wisc.
   B. Winter resorts.
      1. Mustang Island, Texas.
      2. Edisto Island, S.C.
III. America's cut-rate Rivieras.
   A. Lower Rio Grande Valley, Texas.
      1. Climate like Florida; can live on $9 a day or less.
   B. Truth or Consequences, New Mexico.

CONCLUSION

I. Investigate these further, do something different.

ECOLOGY AND PERSONAL WELL-BEING

Broad Subjects

Overpopulation
  Birth control
  *World food problem
  Living conditions
Man and environment
Conservation
Pollution
  Clean air
  Water pollution
  Curbing industrial waste
Distribution of resources
Personal well-being
  *Exercise to keep fit
  *Diet
  How to relax
  *Smoking
  *A philosophy for living
*Charities
*Animal life

* Outlines are developed within these broad subjects.

DEVELOPED OUTLINE

Broad subject: World food problem.
Title: "Can the World Feed Itself?"
General purpose: To inform and persuade.
Exact purpose: To explain the many factors affecting world food production and influence listeners to support methods for achieving more balance of production throughout the world.
Possible audience: Most adult groups, particularly heads of families.

INTRODUCTION

(Testimony)   I. "Famines which are now approaching will . . . last for years . . . and are inevitable. They will sweep areas of Asia, Africa, and Latin America. . . . There is neither a new agricultural method nor birth-control technique which can avert the inevitable famines." From W. and Paul Paddock, *Famine 1975! America's Decision: Who Will Survive?* (1967).

"I should like to unfurl the banner of hope . . . that it now seems possible to win the war against hunger within the next 10 or 20 years." —Secretary of Agriculture Orville Freeman, 1965.

Which of these is correct?

II. Just what is the probability of the world being able to feed itself?

A. Population growth:

(Statistics)   1. 1930 total about 2 billion; 1930–1960 up to 3 billion; 1960–1975 expected up to 4 billion; 2000 expected up to 6 to 7 billion.

B. Let us analyze the situation.

BODY

I. There is an imbalance of food production.

(Problem)   A. U.S. overproduces, yet half the population is undernourished.

   B. Many countries do not produce enough.

(Explanation)   1. Poor growing conditions.
   2. Poor methods of farming.
   3. Inability to pay for imports.

   C. Many factors affect food production.
   1. Soil and climate.
   2. Moisture: natural and irrigated.
   3. Fertilization.
   4. Time factor in planting and harvesting.
   5. Insect and disease control.

II. Methods of correcting imbalance.

(Possible solutions)   A. Export more from productive countries. (develop with examples and statistics)

   B. Bring more land into production.

   C. Improve plant varieties.

(Examples)   1. New types of rice developed in Philippines.
   2. New varieties of wheat developed in Mexico; has now become an exporting country.

   D. Improve livestock production.
   1. U.S. cow can produce 20,000 pounds of milk a year; in some parts of world only 2000 pounds.

   E. Increase effectiveness of fertilizers.

   F. Control insects and plant diseases.
   1. Some countries loss is 25% to 50% of crops.
   2. Can be controlled.

   G. Increased use of irrigation.
   1. Adequate amounts of water are available.

2. Proper use is important.

(Example)
    a. Israel is outstanding example.

H. Increased mechanization.

1. A gradual process.

2. Must recognize that animals dominate in many countries.

I. Education of the farmer.

1. In many of the above methods.

2. Requires help from U.S. and other countries.

III. Foods from the sea a possibility.

A. Great amounts of fish available.

1. 2 billion tons produced in oceans annually.

(Statistics)
    2. Only about 50,000,000 tons caught.

B. Plant growth from sea may become a source of food.

CONCLUSION

I. We are probably not headed for famine in 1975.

II. The situation is serious and will take the concerted effort of experts and the support of all of us in the directions indicated. (Summarize and make final appeal.)

PARTLY DEVELOPED OUTLINE

Broad subject: Exercise to keep fit.

Title: "Should You Jog?"

General purpose: To persuade.

Exact purpose: To influence listeners to take an interest in exercise and to adopt jogging or similar method as an action program.

Possible audience: Older and middle-aged men would be the audience with primary interest. Younger audiences and mixed groups with wives may be interested, with particular adaptation to them in the Introduction and support material throughout the speech.

INTRODUCTION

(Attention and Interest)   I. Hippocrates advanced this law of use 2400 years ago: "That which is used develops; that which is not used wastes away."

A. Applies to the body.

(Testimony)   1. Dr. Paul Dudley White says, "Regular exercise of the large muscles of the body is essential to positive health."

2. Dr. Ernst Jokl, director of Physical Education Research Laboratory, says, "We have discovered an age-inhibiting factor . . . that works like an anti-age antibiotic. It is regular daily exercise."

B. What about you?

(Transition)   II. Let's examine some of the values of regular exercise.

BODY

(Need or
Problem)
(Statistics)

I. Heart attacks are a major cause of death.
   A. Numbers are staggering:
      1. 2,000,000 per year; 1,000,000 deaths.
      2. 55% of all deaths in U.S. are from heart attacks.
      3. Primary group are men from 40 to 60.
   B. Atherosclerosis is cause (hardening of the arteries).
      1. Heart pumps 8000 gallons every 24 hours through 12,000 miles of blood vessels.
      2. "Rust" or coating forms in lining of arteries to block flow.
II. Exercise helps prevent this condition.

(Solution)

   A. American Medical Association Journal says, "Advanced age is not in itself a contraindication to exercise but actually is an indication for it."
   B. Swimming, walking, cycling, running in place, or setting up exercises are all good.
   C. Jogging and walking are particularly good.
      1. First have a physical checkup and consult your doctor.
      2. Start by walking daily, from shorter distances up to four miles a day, or one hour. Perhaps you may not want to jog.
      3. Build up to jogging, first slowly, up to a half hour.
      4. Try running in place, which is advocated by the Air Force. Can be done in a small place.
   D. The added values of exercise include reducing weight, feeling better physically, having a more alert mind.

CONCLUSION

I. Decide what this means to you.

(Action) II. Build a program to suit your needs, body, and interests.

PARTLY DEVELOPED OUTLINE

Broad subject: Diet.
Title: "Keep the Weight Down."
General purpose: To persuade.
Exact purpose: To persuade listeners to realize the value of maintaining correct weight and to diet if necessary.
Possible audience: Most adult Americans.

INTRODUCTION

(Interest
and
Attention)

I. Do you have trouble zipping up your skirt (girls); or buttoning your shirt collar (men)?

II. Much emphasis today on being slim, like "The girl girl-watchers watch."

III. Advent of "miracle drugs" to control weight, as well as many new diet fads and methods.

BODY

(Problem)

I. Being overweight can affect you physically, mentally, and socially.

    A. The physical effects are obvious.
        1. Uncomfortable in clothes.
        2. Sloppy in appearance.
        3. Health effects include high blood-pressure, heart trouble, and effect on other organs, tiredness.

    B. Mental effects more subtle.
        1. Tend to be unwanted and withdraw.
        2. Others are critical.
        3. Develop negative attitudes.

    C. Social effects.
        1. Unattractive to opposite sex.

2. Exclusion from certain groups and social events.

3. Leads to compensatory overeating.

II. Many try to take off weight in harmful ways.

A. Crash or starvation diets, which usually bring only temporary loss of weight at best.

B. Going without breakfast or other meals.

C. Using food substitutes or diet pills.

(Solution) III. Best method is to control intake of food while eating a balanced diet, preferably as advised by a physician.

A. Most experts agree on these principles:

1. Body frame and present weight should be considered.

2. Pace for taking off weight should be realistic.

3. Younger people need more calories than older people.

4. Average man needs about 3000 daily, women about 2000.

5. Reduce intake of calories per day.

6. May eat most of same foods but in smaller amounts, with less starch, fats, butter, etc., depending on the person.

B. Maintain proper balance of nutrients and vitamins.

CONCLUSION

I. Overweight affects us physically, mentally, and socially.

(Action) II. You can bring your weight down, and in proper control, by following these suggestions.

BRIEF OUTLINE

Broad subject: Smoking.
Title: "What Price Smoking?"
General purpose: To persuade.
Exact purpose: To persuade people to stop smoking.
Possible audience: Any group from teen-age to adults, with appropriate adaptation depending on age level.

INTRODUCTION

(Attention and Interest)

I. "What price smoking?"
   A. To your health.
   B. To your pocketbook.
II. Let's examine the status of cigarette smoking.

BODY

(Problem)

I. Recent and growing evidence of effect on health.
   A. Television ads are banned.
   B. Effect on heart and arteries. ⎫
   C. Effect on lungs.   ⎬ (Use recent research data and testimony of health experts.)
   D. Other effects.   ⎭
II. Social and economic effects.
   A. Makes non-smokers uncomfortable.
   B. Cost of cigarettes per pack, day, week, month, year.

(Solution)

III. Many have quit smoking.
   A. Well-known people. (specific examples)
   B. Methods of quitting are available.
      1. Commercial products.
      2. Self-discipline, clubs, and group efforts.

CONCLUSION

(Action)   I. Why not "kick the habit"?
(Appeal)   II. Live a longer, cleaner, less-expensive life.

DEVELOPED OUTLINE

Broad subject: A philosophy for living.

Title: "Live Happily and Long."

General purpose: To persuade (motivate) and inform.

Exact purpose: To motivate for better living by describing the life of Artur Rubinstein as an example to follow.

Possible audience: Would be most appropriate at an occasion such as an anniversary, at a time involving feeling and emotion, to a mixed adult older group; also to a meting or gathering of a music group or organization.

INTRODUCTION

    I. Would you like to be happy on your 84th birthday?

    II. Most of us would settle for happiness and health at a much younger age.

    III. Appropriate reference to the occasion and audience.

    IV. The example of the great pianist Artur Rubinstein is one for all of us.

(Example)   A. NBC produced a 90-minute color TV special about him in 1970.

    B. He has been honored in most countries of the world.

BODY

    I. This is how he lives today.

    A. In his 84th year (1970).

    1. Toured U.S., Europe, Far East, with 104 concerts.

    2. Has given 10 concerts at Carnegie Hall.

(Statistics)   B. Played to 4000 one recent birthday evening.
                       1. At midnight attended birthday party in
                          his honor.
                       2. Alive, twinkling, telling stories, charming
                          the women, drinking champagne.
                    C. Has zest for good and exciting things.
                       1. "Every day brings a new adventure," he
                          says.
(Quotation)   2. "My main residence is the airplane. I
                          love it." Claims he could be a travel
                          agent.
                       3. Can speak 8 languages.
               II. How did this come about?
                    A. Born youngest of seven children in 1890
                       in Lodz, Poland.
(Facts)   B. Married at age 43 the daughter of a Polish
                       conductor.
                       1. In London.
                       2. Children: Eva born in Buenos Aires;
                          Paul in Warsaw; Alina and John in Hol-
                          land.
                    C. Showed music talent early.
                       1. Concert at age five. Debut in Berlin at
                          age 10. Had played in all capitals of
                          Europe by age 15. Debut in N.Y. at
                          age 16.
                       2. Has schedule like a railroad or airline
                          timetable.
                       3. Gave 10 concerts and donated all earn-
                          ings to charity.
                       4. Received Medal of Royal Philharmonic
                          Society in London in 1964, and many
                          other honors and awards.
                    D. Has also seen much tragedy.
                       1. Born into Jewish persecution from Czar-
                          ist Russia in Poland.

2. Saw much suffering of Jews in Europe.
3. Moved in World War II period to U.S.; became citizen.

III. What lessons can we learn?

    A. Optimism as a way of life.

    B. Enjoyment of living for today.

    C. Help and devotion to others.

    D. His own words best reflect his philosophy of life.

(Quotation)

      1. "I simply cannot believe that the culture mankind has accumulated is for nothing. I am an incurable optimist."

      2. "Forget middle-age ailments. Eat four lobsters and caviar, drink champagne. . . . At seventy and eighty there is a wonderful sense of relaxation."

      3. "I will go on playing as long as anyone wants to hear me or until my fingers fail me."

    E. Other leaders in the lighter entertainment areas also reflect philosophies of life all of us can heed.

(Examples)

      1. Louis Armstrong is always happy, smiling, and enthusiastic. He has entertained throughout the world, frequently for charity, always for the happiness of others.

      2. Jackie Gleason, when asked what he would most like to be remembered for, said, "For others to feel that I have helped them toward enjoyment and pleasure."

CONCLUSION

(Develop appropriate to the message, purpose, and occasion.)

BRIEF OUTLINE

Broad Subject: Charities.
Title: "Support the United Fund Drive."
General purpose: To persuade.
Exact purpose: To persuade audience to support the United Fund
 and to contribute to the current drive (in their community).
Possible audience: Adult mixed groups at appropriate occasion.

INTRODUCTION

(Attention   I. Adaptation to audience and occasion.
and   II. Common interest and concern of all in this
Interest)   subject.

BODY

(Problem   I. Many are in need of assistance, despite our
or   affluent society.
Need)   A. National needs. (List areas and types of
              need.)
       B. Local—in our community. (List areas and
              types, using examples and statistics.)
    II. The United Fund helps meet these needs in
       many ways.
(Solution)   A. Underprivileged.
       B. Health and welfare.
          1. Hospitals.
          2. Red Cross and other organizations.
       C. Youth activities.
          1. Scouts.
          2. Others.
(Action)   III. Contributing helps others and gives you per-
       sonal satisfaction.

    A. Builds a better community for all.

    B. Minimizes future needs.

    C. Consider your own good fortune in helping others.

CONCLUSION

(Appeal)   I. Try to give a little more than your usual share.

    II. It will help both you and the community.

BRIEF OUTLINE

Broad subject: Animal life.
Title: "Wild Horses."
General purpose: To inform.
Exact purpose: To present information showing how wild horses are becoming extinct.
Possible audience: Mature adults at appropriate occasion for interest in this subject.

INTRODUCTION

I. The wild horse has been one of our most majestic animals.
II. In today's "horseless carriage" era, he is now facing extinction.

BODY

I. Present status.
    A. Once were 2,000,000 roaming the prairies. Bureau of Land Management estimates only about 16,000 left.
        1. Most in Nevada, Utah, Wyoming, California.
        2. Rare to see a wild stallion majestically watching over his harem of mares.
    B. Being hunted and killed by hunters in airplanes who stampede them, capture, and sell for horse meat at $.06 a pound. One hunter captured 40,000 in 14 years.
    C. Extinction predicted in eight years.
II. Efforts to save them are being made.
    A. International Society for Protection of Mustangs and Burros.
    B. Preserves being established by Bureau of Land Management.
        1. Lovell, Wyoming, 35,000 acres.
        2. Nevada, 300,000 acres.
    C. Recent federal legislation to give Department of Interior full custody failed to pass.

CONCLUSION

I. Much more has to be done to prevent extinction.

THE ECONOMY: CORPORATIONS AND BUSINESS

Broad Subjects

The state of the economy
  The stock market
  *Inflation and controls
  The plight of the consumer
Current status of an industry or company
History of a company
Corporate mergers
*Careers
Unemployment
How to apply for a job
*Small business
*Management improvement
*Instruction and training
Taxes
An unusual success story
The family budget
*The film industry

* Outlines are developed within these broad subjects.

BRIEF OUTLINE

Broad subject: Inflation and controls.
Title: "Are We Ready for Wage and Price Controls?"
General purpose: To persuade (convince on controversial purpose).
Exact purpose: To convince listeners that they should favor the establishment of direct price and wage controls by the federal government.
Possible audience: The subject and purpose are controversial, and the degree of acceptance would depend on the nature of the audience and their present beliefs. A less direct method of presenting the main points is suggested, with sufficient support and proof to be given as needed in leading up to the point.

INTRODUCTION

(Attention and Interest)

I. All are concerned with what our money will buy.

II. Inflation is a major factor in ability to live well on our income.

III. Are voluntary, indirect methods working? What more can be done? (Indirect method; no initial summary of main points except as questions.)

BODY

(Problem)

I. The economy is getting out of hand.
   A. Rising prices.
   B. Rising unemployment. ⎱ (Use latest
   C. Business recession; lower ⎰ statistics and
      profits.   examples)

D. Stock market slump.

E. Hard to borrow money; high interest rates.

II. Methods of indirect control are not working.

(Possible solutions)

    A.

    B.

III. Wage and price controls have worked before.

    A. World War II example.

    B. Korean War example.

    C. The limitations and problems can be corrected.

(Best solution)

IV. We should establish direct controls.

    A. Advantages outweigh the disadvantages.

    B. A workable system can be set up.

    C. This requires cooperation of all.

(Action)

    D. You can help by talking about it and writing your Congressman.

CONCLUSION

I. Summary of points.

II. Unless we act soon, our standard of living will continue downward.

PARTLY DEVELOPED OUTLINE

Broad subject: Careers.

Title: "Should You (Your Husband) Change Careers?"

General purpose: To persuade (stimulate or convince).

Exact purpose: To persuade listeners to keep an open mind regarding their (or husband's) careers and to realize that a change may be beneficial.

Possible audience: This speech should be of primary interest to a mature (40 to 50) age group of men, such as a civic, business, professional, or management. Could be of interest to married women if adapted to them in Introduction. A light after-dinner occasion might be best.

INTRODUCTION

I. What we do for a living concerns us all.

II. Most stay in same career all their lives.

III. Should you consider a change?

BODY

I. If you stay in the same career:
   A. There are advantages.
      1. Security.
      2. Know most about it.
      3. More chance for advancement.
   B. Possible disadvantages.
      1. Boredom.
      2. Too repetitive and "mechanical."
      3. New fields are closed out.

II. There is a trend today toward changing careers, frequently at less income, and due to:
   A. Longer lives.

B. More exciting, dynamic world and environment.

C. Contagious enthusiasm of youth who scorn economic security.

D. Desire for new relaxed or more exciting life.

III. Here are some examples to consider.

A. An Air Force Colonel who worked for a Master's degree and became a college teacher at age 47.

B. A salesman earning $30,000 a year who liked the outdoors. He and wife decided at 16th wedding anniversary to quit and both became high school teachers in Alaska.

C. A veterinarian who longed for physical work and quit to become a shipping clerk in a large department store. His wife also got a job in the store.

D. A Wall Street insurance broker earning $35,000 at age 40. He and wife decided to buy a small inn in Maine, which they run and net only $10,000 a year.

E. A stock broker in a large city quit to study biology, got interested in ecology in early 40s. Studies ocean life and does research and teaching after earning advanced degrees.

F. A store owner in a small town sold out to become a math teacher in the local high school.

CONCLUSION

I. Where do you fit in this picture?

II. Think about it and read a book such as Walter Dukat, *Guide for Professional Careers* which discusses changing careers.

PARTLY DEVELOPED OUTLINE

Broad subject: Small business.

Title: "Small Business Jobs for College Graduates."

General purpose: To inform.

Exact purpose: To inform listeners on trends in seeking employment in small companies by graduates of prestige universities.

Possible audience: College students or recent graduates interested in jobs and future careers, perhaps of students, business and civic clubs or groups.

INTRODUCTION

I. Large companies have traditionally sought top-level employees as future managers from major graduate schools of business.

II. Students of these universities have wanted to go to large companies in the past.

BODY

I. Trend now is toward small companies for employment.
   A. Big company disadvantages.
      1. Too much bureaucracy.
      2. Slow advancement.
      3. Less personal involvement.
      4. "Fortune 500" losing appeal to students.
   B. Small company advantages.
      1. More freedom.
      2. More experiences and involvement.
      3. Make opportunity for leadership.
      4. More rapid advancement and control of one's future.

II. Students of major universities are setting examples.
   A. Harvard University.

1. Students set up Small Business Opportunities International to help seek jobs in small companies.
2. Brochure says, "We want experience and exposure . . . to get our hands dirty."
B. Stanford University.
1. Formed Stanford Small Business Association.
2. "We are trying to stay away from the corporate structure and bureaucracy."
C. Aiming job campaigns at banks, trade, and management associations, and other organizations with contacts with small business firms.
D. They define "small business" as having managements of about 15 and annual sales from $1,000,000 to $20,000,000.

CONCLUSION

I. Harvard's dean, Lawrence E. Fouraker, says of all this, "It's characteristic of the imagination and enterprise of our students."
II. Maybe old-fashioned American small business initiative is on the move again.

PARTLY DEVELOPED OUTLINE

Broad subject: Management improvement.

Title: "Communication in Modern Business."

General purpose: To inform.

Exact purpose: To explain and describe major methods and considerations in accomplishing better communication in today's business organizations.

Possible audience: For specific company groups or general groups of businessmen and managers. The Introduction and examples used would be adapted accordingly.

INTRODUCTION

I. Communication has become a major factor in the management of business.

II. The need is manifest in many ways, including:

    A. Size and complexity of modern organizations.

    B. Technology and specialization.

    C. Information explosion.

    D. Need for consultation.

    E. Participation at all levels.

    F. Morale and employee relations; social climate.

    G. Customer and public relations.

BODY

I. Internal communication: inside the organization.

    A. Methods.

        1. Oral most important: conversation, interviews, speeches, oral reports, conferences, meetings, committees, presentations.

        2. Written: memos, bulletins, newsletters, manuals, reports.

B. Directions.
   1. Up and down organizational channels.
   2. Across or horizontal.
   3. Grapevine and other.
C. Uses and results.
   1. To give and obtain information.
   2. To consult and exchange opinion.
   3. To make decisions.
   4. To train and instruct.
   5. To delegate.
   6. To provide participation opportunities.
   7. To improve morale and relations.
II. External communication: outside the organization.
  A. Public and customer relations.
   1. Speeches, letters, and meetings.
   2. Community and government relations.
   3. Sales meetings.
   4. Customer contacts.
  B. Advertising and promotion.
III. Examples of major company policies and activities in communication.
  A. Chrysler Corporation.
  B. General Electric.
  C. Others.

CONCLUSION

I. Communication in an organization will continue to increase in importance as size, complexity, and need for participation increases.
II. All of these factors (summarize) must be considered.

BRIEF OUTLINE

Broad subject: Instruction and training.
Title: "How to Instruct."
General purpose: To inform.
Exact purpose: To explain and demonstrate the steps in instructing a person to do a job or execute a skill.
Possible audience: One or more persons who will execute the job or skill, either as employees or others.

INTRODUCTION

(Prepare **and** **Motivate)**	I. The need to learn this skill is . . . II. The value of this learning to you is . . .

BODY

	I. The materials and apparatus used in this process.
	A. Show and describe materials.
(Present)	B. Show and describe apparatus or appliances.
	II. The proper setting and positions.
	A. Describe setting.
	B. Describe and show positions.
	III. The specific steps in the process (skill or information to be given).
	A.
	(List steps, explain, demonstrate. Answer questions.)
	B.
	C.

(Apply)

IV. Practice and application by learner.
    A. (Have learner practice and apply each step
    B. and the whole operation. Make corrections
       and suggestions.)

CONCLUSION

(Evaluate)

I. Plan to evaluate and test future performance or knowledge.
II. Summary.

PARTLY DEVELOPED OUTLINE

Broad subject: The film industry.
Title: "The New Movie Producers."
General purpose: To inform.
Exact purpose: To present information on new and unusual investors and producers of movies.
Possible audience: Adult groups who are average movie goers, or business groups interested in new developments.

INTRODUCTION

I. Movies continue to attract our fancy.
II. Trends toward smaller, less-expensive pictures.
  A. By a wide variety of producers.
  B. Low-budget sex films part of trend.
    1. Louis K. Sher, president of Art Theatre Guild, produced "The Stewardess."
    2. Other examples.

BODY

I. Major companies and stars in business are beset with problems.
  A. Expensive films are fewer and hard to finance.
  B. Giants of industry are making shorter movies for TV, etc.
  C. Movie stars such as Frank Sinatra and Gregory Peck have set up companies and are producing movies.
II. Unusual development is the number of people and companies outside the industry who are going into movie production.

(Examples)   A. Mattel, Inc., largest toy manufacturer, produced and financed a $1,000,000 picture, *Where the Lillies Bloom*.

B. Quaker Oats Company producing children's movies.

C. Leon Levy and a partner in Oppenheimer & Company spent only $15,000 on the *Honeymoon Killers* which grossed $1,000,000 in U.S.

D. Real estate and mortgage banking groups loaned $150,000 to Gemini Pictures to make *Which Way Do You Dig* and took a first mortgage on the film to secure the loan.

E. Mercantile Industries, Chicago lending organization, loaned $950,000 to Translook Productions to make *Fools*.

F. Advertising agency, Lois, Holland, Calloway, Inc., are major owners of Saturn Picture Corp.

III. Dissenters question the wisdom of this.

A. Investment firm warns against film financing.

(Testimony)   1. Charles Lewis, of Treves & Company, says, "Anybody who doesn't know the picture business is crazy to invest unless he is very rich or doesn't care."

B. Financing films by large numbers of small backers, as in the theater, is not sound, says Jack O'Connell, a producer.

CONCLUSION

I. All this tends to add up to increasing diversification in movie producers and backers.

II. You may not know where your next movie is coming from.

CONTEMPORARY LIFE STYLES

Broad Subjects

*Buying a used car
 Day camps
 Life on the moon
*Dining out
 Home ownership
    How to finance a home
    Remodeling an old house
    Picking your first home
    Suburban living
    Condominiums vs. homes
*The family budget
 Sex freedom and morals
 Trends in family life
 The new cities
*Making a speech

* Outlines are developed within these broad subjects.

PARTLY DEVELOPED OUTLINE

Broad subject: Buying a used car.

Title: "How to Buy a Used Car."

General purpose: To inform. (Could be persuasive by expanding on point V.)

Exact purpose: To have listeners understand the factors and methods to consider in buying a used car (and to persuade them to buy one).

Possible audience: Almost any group of driving age would be interested, with primary interest for married couples and those in position to purchase cars. Middle- and low-income groups would be most interested.

INTRODUCTION

I. Should you buy a used car?
  A. Car is second-highest investment you'll make.
  B. This is age of second and third cars.
  C. Consider even for your basic car.
II. There are many factors to consider.
  (Make initial summary of points.)

BODY

I. A car is a major investment.
  A. Average American spends $4000 for a new fully equipped car.
    1. Pays largely for depreciation. About 25% first year.
    2. Keeps about 2 to 5 years.
  B. Used cars cost less.
    1. Good used car 1 to 2 years old has depreciated up to 35%. May be in excellent condition.
    2. Older cars depreciate more and may need more repairs.

II. Buying a used car involves some risk.
   A. Trust in dealer or owner.
      1. Not necessarily less risk from dealer. But many guarantee cars.
      2. Owner may be more honest in revealing car's faults.
   B. Amount and type of repair to expect.
      1. Always expect some.
      2. You have a "cushion" in saving from new-car price.
III. Items to consider and check.
   A. General appearance. Evaluate extent of these and cost to repair.
      1. Paint condition.
      2. Body dents.
      3. Rust.
   B. Mileage and maintenance.
      1. Difficult to be sure.
      2. Look at service stickers.
      3. Look at wear on brake pedal and panels in front sides; also floor covering.
      4. New battery is good but may indicate higher mileage than shown.
   C. Tires.
      1. Kicking tires not much of a test.
      2. Relate to odometer mileage.
      3. Original or new? When replaced? Wear evenly?
IV. Mechanical condition.
   A. Motor condition and performance.
      1. Sound of valves.
      2. Smoothness, jerkiness or bucking, acceleration.
      3. Exhaust for oil smoke.
   B. Other items.
      1. Brakes: pedal leverage, performance, pull to side.
      2. Transmission: slipping, shifting.
      3. Wheel alignment: pull to side, tire wear in front.
   C. Test drive.
      1. Yourself if possible.
      2. Take to your mechanic or test center for check.

V. Why not be more daring and try buying a used car next time?
  A. Save major depreciation costs.
    1. Examples.
    2. Data.
  B. Make changes oftener; have more variety.
  C. Enjoy shopping around.
    1. Go to large and small dealers: Reedman's near Philadelphia is largest in the world. Jerome Avenue in New York City mostly wholesale.
    2. Watch the want ads in newspaper.
    3. Bargain and haggle. If not trading a car, offer considerably less than asking price. If trading, you have leeway for bargaining.

CONCLUSION

  I. Consider these points. (make summary)
 II. Maybe you'll become a used-car buyer.

DEVELOPED OUTLINE

Broad subject: Dining out.
Title: "Can You Afford to Eat Out?"
General purpose: To persuade.
Exact purpose: To prove that many restaurants' prices are getting too high and present some suggestions for what to do about it.
Possible audience: A meeting of an organization—either men's, women's, or mixed—in or near an urban area where dining out is a frequent social and business occurrence.

INTRODUCTION

    I. Are you spending more in restaurants and enjoying it less?

        A. Do you feel cheated if each bite isn't exceptionally good?

        B. Is the local Italian restaurant becoming too expensive for you to take your family?

    II. One of our most enjoyable pastimes—eating out —is getting out of reach.

    III. Let's see what causes high prices and what we can do about it.

BODY

(Problem)   I. Restaurants are becoming more expensive every year.

        A. Restaurant costs rising faster than most consumer prices.

(Statistics)   1. Consumer Price Index—restaurant meals up 13.2% in last year.

          2. In New York City area, prices rose 9.4%.

B. Not just high-priced, so-called "snob" restaurants.

(Examples)
1. Soup at Chock Full O'Nuts up 20%—
to 30¢.
2. Frankfurters at Shea Stadium went from
35¢ to 40¢.
3. Good Humor bars are smaller and up to
25¢.

II. Families find dining out prohibitive.

A. Nearly impossible when including the children.
1. Leisure pastime has become luxury.
2. Working mother used to go to Schrafft's
on Saturday with children, but bill rose
to $15 and she had to stop.

B. Working couple with no children feels the
pinch.
1. Used to eat out 2–3 times weekly and
spend $10–$15, says shoe executive's
wife.
2. They still do it, but midtown New York
City restaurants, with drink and tip, are
up to $25 a couple.

III. Who are the villains?

A. Expense account dining.
1. Corporations find it a key part of business day and pay the bills.
2. Thus, few people are paying out of their
own pockets, especially at lunch; restaurants are full and able to charge high
prices.
3. But restaurants suffer because few patrons
pay cash.
a. Supplies must be bought with cash.
b. Many credit-card companies are slow
to reimburse restaurants.
c. Prices are forced still higher.

B. Costs of wine, food, rent, and help are rising.

1. Wine prices rising steadily.

(Statistics)

    a. A $4.50 Beaujolais last year costs restaurants $6 today.

    b. Restaurants set wine prices at twice their cost.

2. Food costs up nearly a third in 3 years.

3. Spiraling rents force many restaurants out of business.

(Solution) IV. Good alternatives to high-priced dining.

A. Search out Chinese, Middle Eastern, or other traditionally less expensive restaurants than French or Italian.

B. Entertain at home.

1. Gourmet clubs, where each guest brings a new dish, are creative, fun, and inexpensive.

2. Many bachelors prefer cooking and hosting dinner parties.

(Testimony)

    a. Says one New Yorker: "I can provide a good curry, dessert, and wine for $10—12 for four."

    b. Dates enjoy helping.

C. Attend a cooking school.

1. In nearly every city.

2. Many specialize in one type of cookery.

D. Hire a catering service or "order out."

1. In all price ranges and types of food.

2. Effortless, original, gives you free time.

CONCLUSION

I. Every time you patronize a high-priced restaurant, remember these facts (summarize main points).

II. Help fight high prices in restaurants by being imaginative and willing to try new foods and ways of dining.

BRIEF OUTLINE

Broad subject: The family budget.
Title: "Stretching the Family Budget" (at supermarket and clothing stores).
General purpose: To inform.
Exact purpose: To present and explain methods of economizing in buying groceries and clothing.
Possible audience: This speech could be given to a group of women, preferably married and with families for maximum interest. Many husbands would also be interested, in a mixed audience.

INTRODUCTION

I. More than 8000 items in the average supermarket.
II. Groceries and clothing are major part of family budget.
III. You can save money by following some simple suggestions.

BODY

I. In buying groceries.
  A. What to buy.
    1. What you need; from a planned list.
    2. Don't go for "specials" unless you can really use them.
    3. Avoid ready-made "convenience" package mixes; cost less to make yourself.
    4. Buy in bulk rather than in boxes.
  B. How to buy.
    1. Alone—not with husband or children.
    2. Don't pick up an item unless you want it.
    3. Check amount as marked in packages and compare.
    4. Watch for freshness.

C. When to buy.
   1. Once a week, not impulsively.
   2. Buy fruits and vegetables in season.
   3. Store quantity bargains in freezer.

II. In buying clothing.
   A. Use a plan—months or a year ahead.
      1. Spend about 10% of income.
      2. Put money aside monthly.
   B. When and where to buy.
      1. Out of and at end of season.
      2. Look for labels you know.
      3. Analyze discount stores for quality.
   C. What to buy.
      1. The best you can afford.
      2. Garments with a double purpose.
      3. Look for tailoring features (stitching, buttonholes, shape).
      4. Get good copies of originals.

CONCLUSION

 I. Be a systematic and careful buyer.
II. Summary: spend your dollars carefully.

DEVELOPED OUTLINE

Broad subject: Making a speech.
Title: "How to Make a Speech."
General purpose: To inform.
Exact purpose: To inform and instruct on the basic principles and methods for making an effective speech.
Possible audience: Any group of adults.

INTRODUCTION

I. All of us are called upon from time to time to make a speech.
II. You should approach this responsibility with a positive attitude by:
  A. Avoiding some of the myths about a speech.
  B. Having a real desire to communicate.
  C. Following a systematic series of steps in preparing by the EXTEMPORANEOUS method.

BODY

I. There are several myths that keep us from making good speeches:
  A. That good speakers are born.
    1. Examples through history refute this. Most good speakers worked hard at it, from Demosthenes to Franklin Roosevelt to . . .
  B. That a speech is an oration or a performance.
    1. No, a speech is natural *enlarged conversation.*
    2. A speech is communication.
    3. Oratory and dramatic performance went out with the turn of the century.

4. Audiences now want to "talk things over" with the speaker, to participate, not to be talked down to by him.

C. That speakers should not be nervous.

  1. All good speakers have nervous energy; also actors, athletes, singers, and all who want to do well before others.

  2. Accept nervous energy as healthy; learn to control it by a positive attitude and good preparation.

D. That elocution and dramatics is good speaking.

  1. No, good speech is not a set of mechanics of voice, gesture, and posture.

  2. Good speech is being one's natural self.

E. That speeches must be read.

  1. Speaking from manuscript, reading, or memorizing do not lead to effective communication usually.

  2. The average speaker should not use a manuscript.

F. Speech is one-way transmittal.

  1. No, speech is communication, which must be an exchange of ideas and meaning with others.

  2. Good speaking requires an understanding of communication as a circular process.

II. Develop a positive attitude.

A. By dispelling all of these myths.

B. By understanding the nature of communication.

C. By desiring to communicate through speaking on subjects and purposes on which you have or can develop knowledge and/or strong beliefs or feelings.

D. By considering your listeners as a major part of the speech process.

III. Follow these steps systematically in your preparation and delivery.

A. Planning: Analyze the nature of the audience in relation to your subject and purpose—their knowledge, interest, beliefs, feelings. Pick the subject carefully and find out as much as you can about it. Narrow this to a general purpose, such as to inform or persuade or both. Then narrow this and state your exact purpose in a sentence.

B. Organizing: Make a list of ideas and points, then narrow this and synthesize into three or four main points for the Body of the speech. Arrange these in best sequence. Make outline of Body, *then* Introduction and Conclusion.

C. Developing: Use best support, development, and proof, including examples, illustrations, statistics, testimony. Consider interest and attention value of all materials and methods. Use clear explanation, description, reasoning, and other methods.

D. Motivating: Consider appeal to listener motives and feelings, to arouse interest and to move to feel, believe, and accept ideas.

E. Communicating: Practice delivery from outline, making notes to be used in the actual speech. Use strong enthusiasm, strong projection, natural manner, gesture, and emphasis as needed.

CONCLUSION

I. You can make an effective speech by following these steps. (summarize)

II. Making a speech is a rewarding and stimulating experience.

TODAY'S YOUTH

Broad Subjects

*General assessment of youth
*Protest and dissent
  Campus unrest
  Youth in the cities
 Military service
 Political activity
  Influence on elections
  Running for office
  Voting
 Summer jobs
*Going to college
*Influence on society

* Outlines are developed within these broad subjects.

DEVELOPED OUTLINE

Broad subject: General assessment of youth.
Title: "Youth."
General purpose: To persuade (stimulate).
Exact purpose: To assess the general status of youth and their needs today.
Possible audience: This outline is made from an essay in the book by Robert F. Kennedy, *To Seek a Newer World* (Doubleday & Company, Inc., 1967), which was developed by him from his speeches on the subject. The outline is in some detail but does not include all of the speaker's support material.

INTRODUCTION

I. The current generation of youth is brighter, better educated, and more motivated than any previous one.
   A. We flatter them by emulating their fashions, slang, music, and dances.
   B. Detroit fashions its cars to those built by teen-age "hot rodders."

II. Yet today we see an alienation of youth in many ways.
   A. Riots on campuses and in cities.
   B. Distrust and rejection of older generation.
   C. Rise in juvenile delinquency.
   D. Group living away from society.

BODY

I. The sources of dissent of the young are many.
   A. The Vietnam war.
      1. Many fight and die.

    2. Others protest and dissent.

    3. There are many and complex reasons.

B. The economy.

    1. Corporations are large part of American life but play small role in solving problems. Some have greater annual profits than the gross national product of any one of 70 nations.

    2. Too much judging success by profit.

    3. Too much materialism and organizational bureaucracy.

    4. Labor unions are too powerful.

C. Education system.

    1. Too much uniformity and tradition of the past.

    2. Suppresses individuality.

D. Political insincerity and distrust.

II. What does all this matter?

A. Youth is rapidly increasing in numbers.

B. Their contributions are sorely needed.

C. Their questioning and criticism reflect on our judgment and confidence in our institutions.

D. Traditional passing on of leadership from older to younger generation no longer is accepted.

    1. Youth respects codes and standards of fellow youth.

    2. Lengthening of formal education has invited greater separation between the generations.

    3. Gulfs yawn between black and white, right and left.

    4. We must have shared aims and goals, along with some confrontation which is good.

III. Other nation's youth are similar; we are not alone.

A. Problem is not unique to America.

    1. Latin America, Europe, Korea, and others.

    2. They may have different complaints in these countries, including more repression.

    3. Communist countries' youth are also resenting the staggering deceits and crimes of totalitarianism.

B. But the American youth is not in a poor and struggling nation; and he need not battle for the right to express himself.

IV. Action is needed.
    A. Gap between generations cannot be completely closed; but it must be spanned.
    B. Youth must feel that change is possible.
      1. That they will be heard.
      2. That there will be some yielding.
    C. Idealism and morality in politics and in the conduct of our lives must be evident.

CONCLUSION

  I. Youth's concern today is the dignity of the individual human being.
    A. They demand:
      1. Limitation of excessive power in the older generations.
      2. A political system that preserves a sense of community among men.
      3. A government that speaks directly and honestly.
    B. We can win their commitment by demonstrating these goals.
 II. We cannot bequeath to the coming generation only the prophetic lament of Tennyson:

> Ah, what shall I be at fifty,
> Should nature keep me alive,
> If I find the world so bitter
> When I am but twenty-five?

PARTLY DEVELOPED OUTLINE

Broad subject: Protest and dissent.
Title: "The SDS Threat."
General purpose: To persuade.
Exact purpose: To persuade and arouse concern over the threat of the Students for a Democratic Society to our youth—particularly in the high schools and colleges.
Possible audience: Parents of high school and college students; also student groups.

INTRODUCTION

(Common ground)

I. All of us are concerned about violence and dissent leading to disruption of our values and a democratic society.

II. A major movement in this direction is the Students for a Democratic Society (SDS) who, by their own manifesto, want to overthrow what we hold dear, by violence and disruption.

III. Most of the points in this speech come from conclusions of the House Committee on Internal Security.

BODY

(Problem)

I. The SDS blueprint.
   A. 1968 Council meeting.
   B. 1969 Organization Manual.
   C. Vietnam position.

II. SDS claims of success.
   A. Ohio State, Columbus, Ohio, summer 1969.
   B. Detroit orientation program, summer 1969.

        C. Akron, Ohio, summer school, 1969.

        D. Pittsburgh, Pa., South Hills High School, September 1969.

        E. Greenville, S.C., November 1969.

   III. Nature of activities.

        A. Using high schools to recruit for later college participation.

        B. Underground press in high schools.

        C. Arouse excitement among students to join.

(Solution)   IV. What can be done about it.

        A. First, understand it and realize it exists.

        B. Plan a defense.

           1. In the schools, with teachers and administrators.

           2. In the home.

CONCLUSION

   I. SDS has established its identity with growing violence and lawlessness.

(Action)   II. We must be alert to this threat and constantly try to thwart it.

BRIEF OUTLINE

Broad subject: Going to college.
Title: "Should They Go to College?"
General purpose: To persuade.
Exact purpose: To persuade parents or high school students to believe that a college education may not be the best training for future job opportunities.
Possible audience: High school students or parents.

INTRODUCTION

(Develop according to audience interest.)

BODY

I. We have automatically assumed a college education is necessary.
  A. For prestige value.
  B. To prepare for life's work.
    1. Still needed for professions and many career opportunities.
    2. But many job opportunities require other kinds of training.
II. Job trends in the 1970–80 decade.
  A. Of all job openings, two-thirds will be in clerical, sales, service, and blue-collar jobs.
  B. These include electronic computer operators, machine operators and maintenance, services of all sorts, cashiers, receptionists.
  C. Some categories to consider; estimated job openings per year.
    1. Manufacturers' salesmen—32,000 jobs per year.
    2. Electronic computer personnel—20,000 per year.
    3. Business machine service—9000 per year.

    4. Plumbers and pipefitters—19,000 per year.

    —U. S. Department of Labor *Occupational Handbook*.

III. Give serious thought to such careers and the kind of training needed. Consider shorter, 2-year programs, junior colleges, vocational schools, etc.

CONCLUSION

(Develop as appropriate.)

PARTLY DEVELOPED OUTLINE

Broad subject: Influence on society.
Title: "Youth in the Next Decade."
General purpose: Inform and stimulate.
Exact purpose: To create an awareness and understanding of the impact of youth today and in the years ahead.
Possible audience: Parents of college and possibly high school age children. Also would be of interest to young audiences to give them an overall picture of their generation.

INTRODUCTION

(Prepare according to adaptation to particular audience.)

BODY

I. Some indicators to watch.
   A. College enrollments.
      1. From 3,500,000 in 1960 to 7,500,000 in 1970.
      2. Will grow to 10,000,000 or more by 1980.
   B. Youth spending for clothes.
      1. Americans spent $50 billion for clothes in 1969.
      2. They spent about $2 billion of this for youth clothes.
   C. Most rapid growing age group is the young.
      1. From 25 to 29 years of age.
      2. In next 10 years, one-third of population will be in 18 to 35 age group.
II. Some future social trends.
   A. Youth morals.
      1. Kinsey found 50% of women virgins at marriage. How much is this outdated?
      2. What effect of coed dormitories and living together in apartments?

   3. What effect of liberal abortion laws? And the pill?
   4. Yet a 1970 AP writer Jurate Kazickas concluded that the pill "has hardly unleashed a wave of indiscriminate sex . . ." and that "coed dorms actually discourage sexual permissiveness . . ."
B. Campus protests and revolts.
   1. What are the real causes, and do they still remain?
   2. After Vietnam, then what?
   3. What effect on high school age groups?
C. Living conditions.
   1. More integration in suburbia.
   2. More high rises and possible slums in suburbia.
   3. Increased traffic problems.
   4. More leisure time.
III. Other influences.
A. Economic.
   1. More young rich and millionaires.
   2. More young in management and executive positions.
B. Political.
   1. Reduced voting age gives great influence to young in elections.
   2. More young elected officials.

CONCLUSION

(Make up appropriate Conclusion.)

PARTLY DEVELOPED OUTLINE

Broad subject: Influence on society.
Title: "Look Behind the Clothes and Listen."
General purpose: To persuade.
Exact purpose: To persuade Americans that the youth of today should not be judged by their appearance, that they are sound and intelligent, and that we are misled by the few who may be bad.
Possible audience: Primarily middle-age and older people. All ages should be interested.

INTRODUCTION

(Attention)

I. Today's youth is accused of much wrongdoing and wrong thinking.
II. We are not the first older generation to be critical of youth.
   A. Ancient Greece and Rome.
   B. Decades of 1920s and 1930s.
III. How much should appearance influence our conclusions about youth?

BODY

(Problem)

I. Many youth choose to appear or dress in "unorthodox" manner.
   A. Long hair and beards. (examples)
   B. Sloppy clothes. (examples)
   C. Gatherings to attract attention. (examples)
II. All this is exaggerated by sensationalism in reporting.
   A. Newspaper pictures and accounts.
   B. Television.
   C. Stores build up beyond realism.

III. We make assumptions and generalizations.

    A. That long hair and beards induce sloppy thinking.

    B. That clothes necessarily "make the man."

    C. That all youth are bad because of the few.

    D. That new ideas are bad.

IV. We should be much more open-minded and not make wrong assumptions.

(Solution)

    A. Actually, most of today's youth are capable and intelligent.

        1. Some 4,500,000 college youth did *not* participate in demonstrations.

        2. College presidents, such as Dr. John W. Oswald of Penn State, and his predecessor, Dr. Eric Walker, say, "I am deeply impressed with the caliber of Penn State students. They are able and concerned. . . . Less than 5% are responsible for starting the demonstrations and riots."

    B. Do not let first impressions cloud objectivity.

    C. Establish and maintain two-way comunication on *their* interests.

    D. Listen to them.

    E. Set an example for them.

CONCLUSION

I. Summary.

(Action)   II. Let's look behind the clothes and listen.

SPEECH PREPARATION CHECK QUESTIONS

1. Is the *exact purpose* stated clearly and concisely at top of outline?

2. Does the *Introduction* arouse interest?
   —Make appropriate adaptation to audience?
   —Short enough?

3. Does *transition to Body* make purpose clear (if desired)?
   —Summarize main points initially (if desired)?
   —Or utilize indirect method (as in controversial persuasion)?

4. Are *main points* few in number?
   —Arranged in best sequence?
   —With appropriate and clear subpoints?

5. Are best *development and support* methods used?
   —Sufficient quantity?
   —Best quality available?
   —Variety in development methods and support?
   —Concreteness and other attention and interest factors used?
   —Appeals to listeners' motives and basic drives?

6. Does *Conclusion* make summary?
   —Indicate future usefulness to audience?
   —Point up advantages and values of proposals if persuading?
   —Show application or action for audience to take?

SOURCES OF MATERIAL FOR SPEECHES

In addition to the suggestions we make in Chapter V for gathering material for speeches, the following lists of references may be useful.

BASIC SOURCES

Newspapers
New York *Times Index*
Magazines
Poole's Index to Periodical Literature
Reader's Guide to Periodical Literature
Radio and television programs
Books
Dictionaries
Encyclopedia Americana, Britannica, and others
Catholic Encyclopedia
Universal Jewish Encyclopedia
Encyclopedia of World Travel
World Almanac
Who's Who in America, and others

OTHER SOURCES

Bartlett's *Familiar Quotations* (Boston, Little, Brown and Company, 1968).

Brussell, E. E., *Dictionary of Quotable Definitions* (Englewood Cliffs, New Jersey, Prentice-Hall, 1970).

Gerler, W. R., *Executive's Treasury of Humor for Every Occasion* (New York, Parker Publishing Company, 1965).

Prochnow, H. V., and Prochnow, H. V., Jr., *The Public Speaker's Treasure Chest* (New York, Harper & Row, 1969).

Roget's (New York, *College Thesaurus,* World Publishing Co., 1962).

SELECTED BIBLIOGRAPHY

Aristotle, *The Rhetoric,* Trans. by Lane Cooper (New York, Appleton-Century-Crofts, 1960).

Berlo, D. K., *The Process of Communication* (New York, Holt, Rinehart and Winston, 1960).

Dance, F. E. X., ed. *Human Communication Theory* (New York, Holt, Rinehart and Winston, 1967).

Holtzman, P. D., *The Psychology of Speakers' Audiences* (Glenview, Illinois, Scott, Foresman, 1970).

Hovland, C. I., Janis, I. L., and Kelley, H. H., *Communication and Persuasion* (New Haven, Yale University Press, 1963).

Kahn, R. L., and Cannell, C. F., *The Dynamics of Interviewing,* (New York, John Wiley & Sons, 1960).

McCroskey, J. C., Knapp, M., and Larson, C., *Introduction to Interpersonal Communication* (Prentice-Hall, 1971).

Nichols, R., and Stevens, L., *Are You Listening?* (New York, McGraw-Hill, 1957).

Oliver, R. T., *History of Public Speaking in America* (Boston, Allyn and Bacon, 1965).

Robert, H. M., *Rules of Order* (Chicago, Scott, Foresman, 1951).

Sturgis, A., *Standard Code of Parliamentary Procedure* (New York, McGraw-Hill, 1966).

Walters, B., *How to Talk with Practically Anybody about Practically Anything* (New York, Doubleday & Co., Inc., 1970).

Zelko, H. P., *The Business Conference* (New York, McGraw-Hill, 1969).

Zelko, H. P., and Dance, F. E. X., *Business and Professional Speech Communication* (New York, Holt, Rinehart and Winston, 1965).

INDEX

speech planning, 51–52; and developing ideas, 93, 96–98; differences in as barrier to communicating, 40–41; and group discussion, 168; motivation, persuasion and selling, 99–113; and organization of ideas, 69, 71–72; and selection of subject for speech, 55

File (speech file), 62

Film industry, as speech subject, 308–9

"Financial Plight of Colleges and Universities," outline for speech on, 206–8

Foreign countries, as speech subject, 234–35

Forums, public, 171–73; seating arrangements for, 172–73

Frames of reference, individual: communication and, 11, 39

Frizzell, John Henry, 17–18

Frost, David, 135

Future of the universities, as speech subject, 206–8

Gavin, William, 131

Generalizing (generalization), use of, 108–9, 139. *See also* Overgeneralizing

Gestures, use of, 118, 123

Goals (purposes) of communication, 6–7; in business conferences, 174; and determining exact purpose of speech, 56–61; and extemporaneous speaking, 16–18; listening and determination of, 30–31, 142–43; motivation, persuasion and selling, 30–31, 99–113; organization of ideas and, 63–83; planning of speech and, 50, 54; preparation of speech and, 185; relationship of speech title to, 58–60; work performance interview and, 166

Government and community affairs, as speech subject category, 189, 191–210

Great men, as speech subject, 198–99

Group discussion(s), 159, 160, 168–79; business conferences, 173–79; committees, 173; dynamics of communication and, 168; forums, 171; meetings and parliamentary procedure, 169–70; motions, table of, 170; panel, 171–73; public, 171; social and family, 168–69; suggested discussion outline for, 171

Hearing, distinguished from listening, 137. *See also* Listening

"Hemline War," outline for speech on, 220–21

Henry, Patrick, 51, 92

Hickel, Walter, 159

Hitler, Adolf, 111

Hoover, Herbert, 3

Hope, Bob, 91

"Houseboats: A New Living Experience," outline for speech on, 275–76

"How Far Can Russia Be Trusted?"—outline for speech on, 192–94

"How Sugar Is Produced," outline for speech on, 250–51

"How to Buy a Used Car," outline for speech on, 312–14

"How to Instruct," outline for speech on, 306–7

"How to Make a Speech," outline for speech on, 320–22

Human communication, 33–45 (*see also* Communication); barriers to, 34, 39–45, 137–40; encoding-decoding process in, 37–38, 39, 44; factors influencing effectiveness of, 33–35, 39–45; good principles and techniques for, 34–35; intrapersonal, 38; listening and, 34, 35–39, 40–45; meaning and, 39; modern theory of, 35–37; nature of, 38–39; process of, 34

Humor, use of, 85, 95, 147, 152, 154–55

Humphrey, Hubert H., 12, 21, 26

"I" (self-centered) attitude versus "you"-centered approach, as barrier to communication, 32, 35, 39, 101, 110, 140, 161

Ideal (model) speaking, 14, 118

Ideas, development and organization of, 63–83, 84–98, 185–86; attention and interest factors, 85, 95–96, 99–113, 123, 186; body of speech and, 71, 80, 82; conclusion of speech and, 80, 82–83; introduction of speech and, 80, 81–82; main ideas, 64–70; outlining, 78–83; and patterns of speech organization, 71–83; and practice in delivery of speech, 119–21; and problem-solving, 75–78; steps in, 64; support forms and tools, 85–93, 96–98, 186; to inform, 63–64, 72–74; to persuade, 69, 74–78; visual aids and, 93–95, 97

Illustrations, use in development of ideas of, 88–90, 97

Image of speaker, impact on listeners and, 9, 10–11, 13, 21, 33, 104, 109. *See also* Self (mental attitude)

Imagery, use in language of, 147, 186

Impromptu speaking. *See* Extemporaneous (impromptu) speaking

Indirectness, suggestion and persuasion and, 110

tion, 33; motivation and concern for, 101–4; preparation in speechmaking of, 26–30; speaker's, impact on listeners and, 9, 10, 13, 26–30, 39, 122

Self-centeredness, and communication, 32, 35, 39, 101, 110, 140, 161

Self-discipline, listening and, 138, 140–42

Self-esteem, motivation and appeal to, 103

Self-preservation, motivation and appeal to, 102

Selling: defined, 100; motivation, persuasion and, 99–113; as persuasion, 111–13; persuasive interview for, 165

Selling of the President 1968, The (McGinniss), 128–29

Sense stimulation (sensory appeal), motivation and, 104, 186

Sentiment(s), motivation and, 103–4

Setting(s): as factor in effective communication, 32–34, 42; informal and group communication and, 159, 160, 168; practicing speech delivery and, 120–21; and purpose of speech, 57; special occasion speaking and, 147–58

Sex drive, motivation and, 103

"Should Movies Be Censored?"—as speech subject, 257–62

"Should They Go to College?"—outline for speech on, 329–30

"Should You (Your Husband) Change Careers?"—outline for speech on, 300–1

"Should You Jog?"—outline for speech on, 285–87

Similes, use of, 89–90

Small business, as speech subject, 302–3

Smoking, as speech subject, 290

"Sniffing—a Dangerous Drug Habit," outline for speech on, 263

Social discussion, 168–69

Social problems, as speech subject category, 189, 253–67

Socrates, 134

Source material for speeches, 61–62, 336

Space (spacing) of points in speech to inform, 73

Speaking and listening rates, communication and, 43–44, 139

Special occasion speeches, 147–58; after-dinner, 153–56; banquets (dinners), 149–53; briefings and presentations with visual aids, 156–57; chairmen or toastmasters at, 149–53; impromptu speaking, 158; introducing speakers, 152–53; praise or eulogy, 148–49; presentation and acceptance of

awards or honors, 147, 148; welcome and response, 149

Speech file, building of, 62

Speechmaking, as speech subject, 320–22

Speech organization, patterns of, 71–83

Speed rates of speech and listening, difference in, 43–44, 139

Statistics, use of, 90–91, 97, 124–25

Status: differences in and communication, 40, 168; and motivation, 102–3

"Status of Public School Education," outline for speech on, 204–5

Stereotype thinking, 138–39

Stevenson, Adlai E., 12, 16

Stimulating (stimulation): attentive listening and, 135, 136 (*see also* Attention factors and qualities); in conferences, 177; persuasion and, 104, 105, 186

Stories (anecdotes), use of, 90, 155

"Stretching the Family Budget," outline for speech on, 318–19

Subject(s), selection of, 53–55; categories for outlines, 189; organizing main ideas and, 64–70; relation to speech purposes and, 59–61; source material, 61–62, 336; and speech preparation, 185; suggested topics, 54–55, 183–325 *passim*

Suggestion: indirectness, persuasion and, 110

Support methods and tools, development of ideas and, 85–93, 96–98, 186

"Support the United Fund Drive," outline for speech on, 294–95

Survival, motivation and concept of, 102

Synthesis (synthesizing) process, organization of ideas and, 66–69

Tact, discussions and, 162–64

Tape recorder, use of, 121

Technical words, avoidance of, 45

Technology and science, as speech subject category, 189, 241–51

Television: delivery, adapting to, 128–31; programming quality as speech subject, 270–71

Testimony, use in development of ideas, 91–93, 95–96, 97, 124–25; cumulative effect of, 96, 97

Thinking (thought processes), 106–9; listening and, 137–40; logical or straight 106–9 (*see also* Logic); mental tools and, 142–43; problem-solving group discussions and, 171–73

"This is nothing" method, organization of ideas for persuasion and, 75, 77–78

Time (chronological) sequence, speeches to inform and, 73